COW - KEEPING IN INDIA

Owing to the antiquity and rarity of this book, certain pages are regrettably absent, and readability is compromised due to the blurring of the original text. If you possess any insights regarding the availability of these missing sections, kindly inform us. Your assistance is crucial in ensuring the completion of this significant work for the benefit of future generations.

COW - KEEPING IN INDIA

A SIMPLE AND PRACTICAL BOOK ON THEIR CARE AND TREATMENT, THEIR VARIOUS BREEDS, AND THE MEANS OF RENDERING THEM PROFITABLE

ISA TWEED

GYAN

Published by

GYAN

Gyan Publishing House
5, Ansari Road
Daryaganj, New Delhi-110002
Phone: 011-47034999, 9811692060
E-mail: books@gyanbooks.com

Distribution Network
gyanbooks.com
India, USA, Canada, UK, Australia

ISBN: 978-93-6780-807-8 (PB)

First Published, 1900

2nd Impression 2024

Printed at: Gyan Press, Delhi.

COW - KEEPING IN INDIA
Author: ISA TWEED

Hansi Cow.

COW-KEEPING
IN INDIA.

A Simple and Practical Book on their Care and Treatment, their various Breeds, and the Means of rendering them Profitable.

BY

ISA TWEED,

AUTHOR OF "POULTRY-KEEPING IN INDIA."

WITH FORTY ILLUSTRATIONS.

SECOND EDITION.

CALCUTTA AND SIMLA:

THACKER, SPINK & CO.

LONDON: W. THACKER & CO., 2 CREED LANE, E.C.

1900.

PREFACE.

WHEN I commenced keeping cows I often wished for a simple and practical book on cattle and their care and treatment in India, and I have frequently heard the same wish expressed by others. If I had had such a book I would have been saved a great deal of needless worry and loss.

There are many books on cattle and their care in Europe; but though these books are a great help to people in Europe, they are of no practical use to us in India. The climate and soil of India are different from those of England and other European countries, and the cattle here need different treatment. Some books have been published on Indian cattle, but the best of these is far from being complete.

I have for the past eighteen years kept my own cows; and for many years have myself undertaken their medical treatment. I have also carefully read all the books I could procure on cattle of all descriptions, both English and Indian.

The knowledge I have thus acquired may be of some service to others, so I herein give my experience for what it may be worth.

The method of treatment that I herein recommend, for cows in health and sickness, is what I have most successfully adopted for many years. I generally adhere to homœopathy, and in most cases it is the only effectual method of treatment; but in many cases I have found the native remedies very efficacious. I do not hesitate to prescribe the most effective remedy, be it homœopathic or native medicine, or anything else.

As I have said, I have carefully read many books on cattle, their diseases and treatment; and in my notes I have tried as much as possible to avoid even the appearance of plagiarism. But it is impossible for any two persons writing on one subject, and especially a subject like this, to avoid often saying the same thing, and sometimes saying it in the same words.

Amongst the first things I learned when I commenced life were: 1st, if I wished to succeed in anything, I must do the work myself and not trust another person to do it for me; 2nd, I must attend to every detail with equal fidelity. As with other matters in life so with the keeping of cows, personal care and supervision, and the strictest attention to details, are absolutely essential to success. The least negligence or delay will cause much loss and disappointment. If a person has not the inclination or time to look after his pets and live stock, he should not attempt to keep any.

The busiest people need regular recreation from their regular work. Without it, it is impossible to maintain good health or mental equilibrium. The greatest minds have experienced this, and it is hazardous to ignore this rule of health. Some persons choose gardening or carpentry as a recreation, others, again, riding or some game of sport. But keeping cows is a very healthful and, at the same time, profitable pastime.

I have often thought, if more European and well-to-do native families in India were to keep cows there would be less disease, and less annoyance about procuring pure milk, butter, and ghee, and there would also be a great improvement in the breed of cattle. Keeping cows does not take much time or money, if one knows how to do it properly. But this knowledge is not acquired without careful study and some experience.

I am convinced that very few persons in India know how to properly care for cattle when in health, or treat them when sick. Most people trust the care of their cattle entirely to their servants, and believe every word the stupid and dishonest gowallah says. I have seen many splendid cows utterly spoiled, and a number die from sheer neglect or mismanagement.

There are a number of good Veterinary Surgeons and gentlemen practising medicine in every town, and it would be more economical in the end to consult the best of them than to trust the stupid native servants.

ISA TWEED.

1890.

PREFACE TO SECOND EDITION.

IT is gratifying to know this book has been well received by the public, and has been a help to a large number of persons. In this the second edition I have made only such corrections and additions as I find after further experience to be necessary. I trust this book will continue to do its good work.

ISA TWEED.

1899.

CONTENTS.

BOOK I.

LIST OF ILLUSTRATIONS.

COW-KEEPING IN INDIA.

CHAPTER I.

THE ADVANTAGES OF KEEPING COWS.

SOME persons keep cows for pleasure, some from necessity, and others as a matter of business. Whatever the object may be, cow-keeping can be made profitable.

Pure Milk.—The first advantage derived from keeping one's own cows is, you get pure milk. Pure milk is very essential to health; some persons do not drink milk, but they eat butter and ghee. If the milk be impure the butter and ghee made from it must also be impure. If people do not think of their own health, and are willing to poison themselves by drinking impure milk and eating infected butter and ghee, they should at least have some thought for the health of their families and friends, who may not be quite so anxious to suffer and die.

Too much stress cannot be put upon the necessity for having pure milk; but it is impossible to procure such an article from the gowallahs or low caste natives.

If people only knew what milk obtained from most of the gowallahs contained, I am sure they would never more drink such stuff. Many gowallahs are not at all scrupulous about the quality of water they put into the milk. I have seen them dip their dirty clothes into stagnant filthy pools and wring the water out into the milk they are carrying to their customers; I have also seen them wash their hands in the milk. Many of them adulterate their milk with chalk and water, finely-sifted flour and water, yellow sugar, *batasha* and water, and innumerable other things that only the gowallah's ingenious mind could suggest. I have known some enterprising spirits among them to dilute Swiss tinned-milk with water, and adulterate their milk with it. Some add water to buffalo's milk to bring it to the consistency of cow's milk, and mix this with the latter. Buffalo's milk being very thick, a lot of water has to be added to it to make it as thin as cow's milk. Mashed plantain is largely used for mixing with butter.

These admixtures cannot but prove extremely injurious to the health of the consumer. It is exceedingly difficult for Europeans to guard against these dangers, especially when their servants are leagued together with the gowallahs.

Cheapness.—The second advantage gained by keeping cows is, cheapness. The daily cost of feeding and keeping a cow should not exceed three-fourths the price of the milk she gives. If she gives six *seers* of milk per day, and the price of milk be one anna per *seer*, her food and keep should not cost more than four and a half annas per day. In some places fodder and grain are very dear, but milk is also proportionately dear in these places. For instance, in Calcutta the price of good milk is one rupee for six *seers*; so if a cow gives only six *seers* a day in Calcutta, it is not too much to spend from six to eight annas a day on her food and keep. A large cow, properly fed and giving from nine to twelve *seers* of milk, should never cost more than eight annas a day for her food and keep even in Calcutta.

It is always more profitable to keep a cow giving a large quantity of milk, than one that gives only a small quantity. A good large cow will give from ten to twelve *seers* a day, and the cost of her keep and food will not exceed from a fourth to a third of the value of her milk. The surplus milk can be sold, or made into butter and ghee for home use or for sale. Milk, butter, and ghee will always find a ready sale. Thus there need not be the least waste.

Calf.—Besides the profit from the milk, there is the calf. If the calf be of a good breed, at eight or ten months of age it will sell for from ten to twenty rupees.

Other Produce.—Then, again, there is the dung. The natives make a great deal of profit from this article. The dung should be gathered every day, and preserved for either fuel or manure. It should be made into cakes or rolls, and dried and sold as fuel, or else, a pit should be dug and the dung and urine thrown into it every day. Cow-dung and urine make splendid manure. The dung of one cow should fetch from eight annas to one rupee a month.

There is money even in the hide, horns, and bones of the cow when she dies.

If the cow be left to the care and mercy of native servants, she will soon become a troublesome and expensive thing, whereas the wicked servants will reap the profit from her.

Keeping Cows is a Pleasure and a Saving.—By having my own cows I have good milk and butter, and for less than I would have to pay for inferior milk and butter bought from the gowallah.

The wife of a military officer who has lived many years in India, writes: "A twenty years' experience, during which I have kept a record of every cow bought and sold, and every calf born, enables me to assert that cows properly looked after are an economy. A cow purchased is, if well managed, so much capital; a calf born is so much increase on your capital, and the cost of the mother's feed and keep is more than balanced by the milk and butter she supplies. I have kept cows in the hills and in the plains, and I have also been without cows, and my account books show that I have paid more for milk and butter when I bought them, than I expended in the food and keep of my cows when I had them, and that in the latter case there was always plenty of dairy produce and to spare, whereas when I had to purchase, milk and butter had to be obtained sparingly and expended carefully. This is a great consideration in a large family, where, for the sake of the young people, milk and butter should be generously given out."—*Cows in India.*

FIG. 2.—HANSI HEIFER.

CHAPTER II.

BREEDS OF CATTLE.

There are several distinct breeds of cattle in India. To ensure success in the dairy and farm, it is of the utmost importance that the best milking breeds of cattle be selected.

Some people are penny-wise and pound-foolish, and will buy cows of no breed whatever and of very inferior milking qualities, rather than pay a decent price for a thoroughbred and good cow. An inferior cow can be bought for a few rupees, but she will give little or no milk, and her food and keep will cost more than her milk is worth. Besides, her calf will sell for hardly anything. This is a great loss. It is always more profitable to keep a good large cow that will give the required amount of milk, than to keep three or four inferior ones that will in the aggregate give that quantity. Four inferior cows will cost more to feed and keep than one or two good ones will. And the one or two good ones can be given better care and attention than it is possible to give the three or four inferior

Fig. 3. Hansi Bullock.

Fig. 4. Hansi Bull.

ones; and without proper care and treatment no cow will give much milk.

I will now endeavour to describe the principal breeds of cattle in India.

Hansi or Hissar.—Hissar and Hansi are neighbouring districts in the North-West Provinces. The breed of cattle found in these districts is thought a great deal of. They stand from 56 to 64 inches high; their heads are broad, necks short, humps high, hips broad, and hind quarters square; they carry their heads erect, and have long curved horns inclined backward, and thin long tails; they are of great substance and have long bodies, deep wide chests, and massive and rather short legs fairly apart to support the carcase. The bullocks are very large and strong, and draw great weights and heavy ploughs, but are not so fast as bullocks of some other breeds. They are generally of a nice white colour, but sometimes red, black, brown or piebald ones are found. These cattle are exceedingly handsome.

In their own districts the cows give from ten to sixteen *seers* of milk in twenty-four hours, but when removed from the fine pasturage of Hissar their milk somewhat decreases. The milk is of the best quality, generally of a creamy white colour.

In their own districts these cows sell from Rs. 40 to Rs. 80 each, and the bullocks from Rs. 60 to Rs. 150 each. In Calcutta they will sell for double the above prices.

Fig. 5.—Nagouri Cow.

Nagourie.—The Nagourie cattle are said to be natives of Nagpore, in the Central Provinces. In former days they were largely bred at Delhi, but now they are seen all over the North-West and Central Provinces.

The cows are very gentle, and give from ten to sixteen *seers* of milk a day, but the milk is not very rich.

Nagourie cattle are of the well-known trotting breed; the bullocks are much prized, and used by native gentlemen for their carriages. Nearly half a century ago they were extensively used in the large cities by rich native gentlemen, and in those days were carefully bred for the purpose, but now they are not so well preserved, and good cattle are scarce.

These cattle are very tall and narrow; some of them measure 64 inches in height. They have long curved horns, long and narrow heads, and a round bump stands out between their horns; their humps are high and narrow; their hind quarters are narrow; their tails are long and thin, with a thick and long bunch of black silky hair on the end. Their hoofs and pasterns are long, and this enables them to trot so well. They are not very fleshy, lacking the great substance of the Hissar breed. The pace of these bullocks is nearly equal to that of a good trotting horse, but they are not able to draw heavy burdens; their carriages are much like light ekkas, with two wheels, and pole tilted up to prevent any weight falling on the back of the bullocks.

FIG. 6.—NELLORE BULL.

They are of a bluish white colour, and are the most delicate cattle in India.

Good cows of the pure breed sell from Rs. 60 to Rs. 100 each, and good trotting bullocks from Rs. 200 to Rs. 400 each.

Like the Hansi, they are not very prolific, but milk for a long time.

Nellore.—Nellore is in the Madras Presidency. This breed has long been celebrated for the milking qualities of the cows, and the great strength and spirit of endurance of the bullocks, on account of which they fetch large prices.

A good specimen of the Nellore breed is a huge animal standing from 60 to 64 inches in height, with a noble look, and very gentle and slow in its movements. It is readily recognised by its form and horns. The horns are hardly ever longer than from three to six inches, and are inclined outward, tapering to a blunt point; the animal has a dull countenance and large, prominent, and heavy-looking eyes; its face is short and its forehead and muzzle broad; its ears are large and lopping; its eyes, hoof, and tail tuft are black; it carries its head erect, and has a short stout neck rising over the withers into a huge hump, which frequently inclines to one side; its back is short and straight; its chest is fairly deep and wide, and its carcase compact and solid-looking, with a heavy dewlap; its legs are

FIG. 7.—NELLORE HEIFER.

clean and massive, straight and fairly apart to support the body; its skin is fine and covered with soft short hair. The prevailing colour is white.

The cattle of this breed generally are heavy-looking creatures, but there is a tendency in some of them to grow tall and leggy. The bullocks draw (a pair of them) thirty *maunds* in a cart, and are excellent for the plough.

The price of a pair of bullocks ranges from Rs. 150 to Rs. 350. The cows give from ten to fourteen *seers* of milk a day. The milk is very rich; good cows sell for from Rs. 100 to Rs. 300 each.

Guzerati or *Surati*—sometimes called Kuttywari.

Guzerat and Surat are in the Bombay Presidency. This breed of cattle is somewhat similar to the Hissar in height, form, and substance, and the cows are very good milkers. They have smaller horns and larger ears than the Hansi, and most of those I have seen have not such large humps.

The bullocks are large, strong, and heavy, and do well in the plough, and draw heavy burdens. These cattle sell for from Rs. 60 to Rs. 200 each.

Goorgaira, in the Mooltan district, produces another good breed of cattle. The cows have all the good qualities of the Hissar, but are not so large or so delicate as they are. They are middle-sized and handsome, broad and well-knit, and of a dark colour. Some of the

FIG. 8.—GUZERAT COW.

best have black points. They are hardy and healthy, and beautiful milkers. Their horns are not very long.

A cow gives from eight to ten *seers* of milk a day, and fetches from Rs. 30 to Rs. 60 in her own district.

Sind.—I have seen some very fine cows from this part of the country. In size and form they are very much like the *Goorgaira.* Those I have seen were a pretty fawn with white points. Some of them are very good milkers.

Mysore Bullocks. — Besides the above-mentioned principal breeds of milk and draught cattle, the Amrit Mahal breed of Mysore are very excellent bullocks; but the cows are no good as milkers, they rarely give more than two *seers* of milk a day.

These bullocks are noted for their great strength and powers of endurance. They rarely exceed 60 inches in height, and generally are only about 48 inches; but in proportion to their size they are remarkably deep and wide in the chest, long and broad in the back, round in the barrel, well ribbed up, and strong in the shoulders and limbs.

They are active and fiery, and some of them walk faster than the troops; they generally have straight horns from two to three feet in length, tapering and sharp-pointed, inclining forward, and slightly approaching each other at the top; their countenance is sprightly; their eyes are large, black, and prominent, expressive

FIG. 9.—GOORGAIRA COW.

and full of fire; they have long and moderately narrow faces; their muzzles and hoofs are black; they carry their heads erect on a moderately-sized and well-formed neck; they have fair-sized humps and small dewlaps. The cows are generally white, but the bulls are grey; some are dark coloured.

A good bullock will fetch from Rs. 100 to Rs. 150 in its own district.

Bengali Cattle.—In Bengal there is no special breed of cattle. The best specimen is a cross-bred between a cow of the district and a bull of one of the above-mentioned breeds.

A few years ago, some Hissar bulls were brought to Burdwan in order to improve the cattle. Also at Soori and Bankipore, some Europeans of the districts took great interest in the improvement of cattle, and imported some fine Hansi and English bulls. But not many of the ryots appreciated this, and when the bulls died, no efforts were made to import new ones.

In different parts of the country some rich Zemindars have imported a few Hansi or half-bred bulls and let them loose as Brahmini bulls. The animals roam about all over the place, and the ryots are allowed their services; but even in such cases, very few persons take any pains to improve their cattle. Nevertheless, as the result of these crosses, some of the best cattle in Bengal are found in the Burdwan, Soori, and Bankipore districts.

FIG. 10.– MYSORE BULLOCK.

The Government should take up this matter, and import good Hissar bulls into all the districts of Bengal. Every village or group of villages should be induced to purchase and keep a bull, and the people should be encouraged to improve their cattle, by offering them prizes for the best specimens, and having cattle shows.

The villagers should be made to pay something towards the purchase and keep of the bull, then they will take a greater interest in the animal, and will take some care of him. The bull should be put in the care of the headman of the village, and he should be responsible to the magistrate for its proper treatment. If this plan were adopted throughout Bengal, in five years there would be a very marked improvement in the cattle.

In Calcutta, there are very few thoroughbred bulls, but a number of half-bred ones are kept for breeding purposes.

The best bullocks for the plough and cart in Bengal are the cross-bred—between the half-bred country cows and thoroughbred Hansi or Nellore bulls—that is, of the second crossing.

Cattle deteriorate very much in the hands of the ryots of Bengal. The thoroughbred large cattle are too delicate, and need much more care than the ordinary Bengali villager is able or inclined to give them. But the cross-breds are very strong and hardy, and the people prefer them.

FIG. 11.--CROSS HANSI COUNTRY.

Cross-breds are found all over India, especially in the North-West Provinces. Some of them are excellent milkers, and are more hardy than the pure breed. They sell for from half to three-fourths of the price of cows of pure blood.

A half-bred Bengali cow will give from four to six *pucca seers* of milk a day, and will sell for from Rs. 20 to Rs. 60. A half-bred bullock will stand about 48 inches high, and will sell for from Rs. 80 to Rs. 150 per pair.

The ordinary Bengali cattle are very small and weak, measuring from 32 to 42 inches in height, and sell for from Rs. 6 to Rs. 12 each. The bullocks cannot do much in the cart or at the plough, and the cows give from a quarter of a *seer* to two *seers* of milk a day.

Darjeeling Cows.—There is a breed of cattle I have seen at Darjeeling; I am not able to say if it is an indigenous breed, or if it is a cross between the cows of the district and English bulls. Some of the cattle look very much like English ones; others again look like wild cattle. They are large, about the size of English cows, and have long hair and horns; some have moderately large humps, others again have none. They are generally black, or red, or piebald; some of them are exceedingly handsome. The bullocks are very strong, and the cows give about six *seers* of milk a day. I doubt if these cattle would live in the plains.

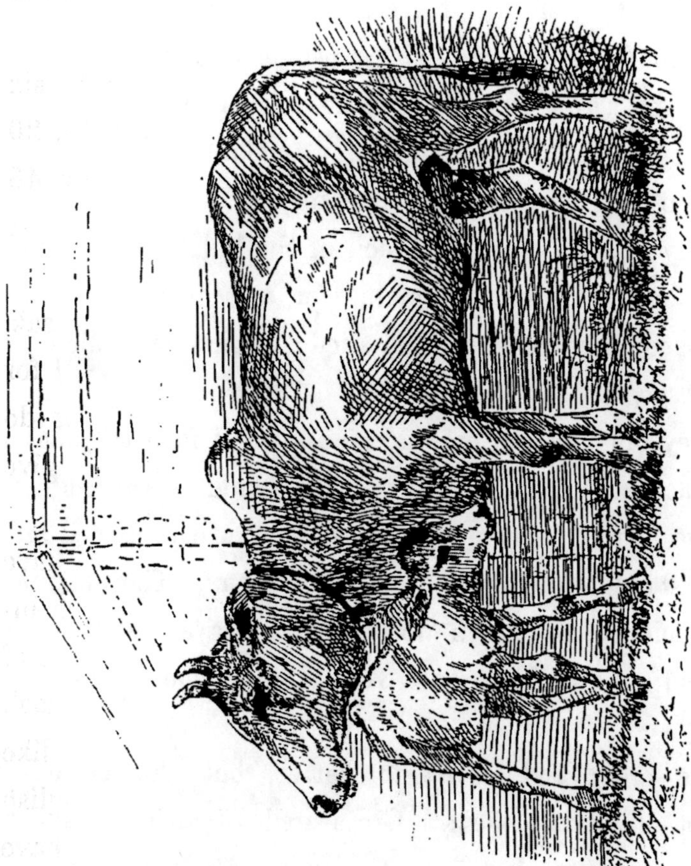

Fig. 12.—Bengali Cow.

English Cattle are not a success in India. They suffer much from the heat, and the milk greatly decreases; not many are able to give them the care and attention they need. Nevertheless, some people prefer them to Indian cows. If a person has a large cool house and a few biggahs of land with many trees and a tank on it, and can afford an attendant for each cow, then he may keep them successfully.

They do not suffer so much in the hills. Some cows have done well on the plains for a year or two, and then suddenly sickened and died; others have died in the first year.

They must be fed on the same kind of food they have been accustomed to in their native land. Any sudden change in food may prove injurious. Mustard-seed oil-cake should never be given to them. They should have plenty of green food. I always look upon English cows in India as a very troublesome and costly luxury.

The cross-bred cows do better, but the bullocks cannot stand the heat. Cross-bred English cows are found all over India, especially in Madras, parts of Bombay, and the North-West Provinces and the Punjab. English cows should be crossed by Hissar, Nagouric, Guzerati, and Nellore bulls; and Hissar, Nagouric, Guzerati, and Nellore cows should be crossed by short-horn bulls. I have always found crosses between the

FIG. 13.—DARJEELING COW.

above-mentioned bulls of India and English cows better than those obtained from English bulls and Indian cows.

The Durham shorthorn cows are the best, and the Suffolk cows the next best for dairy purposes. The Ayrshire and Jersey cows are also very excellent. The Devon and Jersey produce the best cream and butter.

Other Breeds.—The Bhagalpoori cattle are not thought much of. The bullocks generally are too long-legged and weedy, and the cows do not give more than five *seers* of milk a day.

The Gainee is a very pretty miniature breed of cattle; they are kept as fancy pets. They are too small for work, and the cows give very little milk. They are not larger than a large-sized goat. There is as much difference between a full-sized Gainee and a Hansi bull, as there is between a toy terrier and a mastiff.

The Breed to get.—If a person wishes to keep cows for the use of his own family, he should purchase one, two, or three (or as many as he requires) thoroughbred cows of the Hissar, Nellore, Guzerati or Goorgaira breed; or else, good cross-breds of the second crossing between the cows of the country and bulls of pure blood. No cow giving less than 1500 *pucca seers* of milk in the year is worth the trouble and expense of keeping. Some cows will give from 2000 to 3000 *seers* of milk from the time they calve to the time they run dry. I

Fig. 14.—Shorthorn Dairy.

have been told of a Hansi that milked for twelve months, and gave more than 4000 *seers* of milk in that time.

If a person wishes to keep a dairy-farm, he must keep cows that give the largest quantity of milk, and will have to pick them from all breeds.

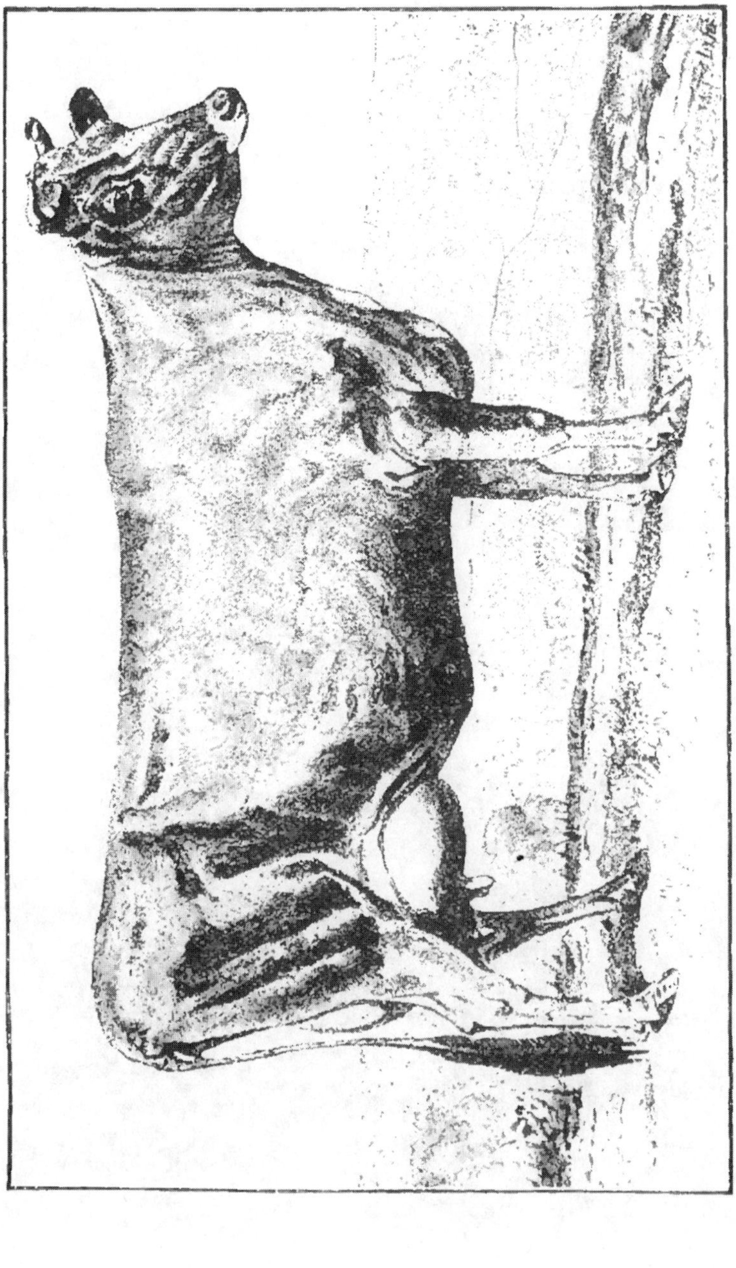

FIG. 15.—JERSEY.

FIG. 16.—SUFFOLK COW.

FIG. 17.—AYRSHIRE COW.

Fig. 18.—Half English Cow.

Fig. 19.—Cross Devon and Nellore.

CHAPTER III.

BUYING COWS.

Quantity of Milk required.—Before buying cows, a person should first consider how much milk he will require daily. Then he will know exactly how many cows he needs to buy.

If a cow in full milk gives ten *seers* of milk a day, she will average seven *seers* per day for nine months, and will remain dry for four or five, and sometimes six months. A good cow, with proper care, should give a calf every fifteen or sixteen months. Calculate accordingly, and see how many cows you need to keep you regularly supplied with the required quantity of milk.

If wanted for the use of the family, and if no cow has yet been purchased, I would advise the adoption of the following plan. To begin with, buy only one cow in full milk; five months later buy another one, and a third one another five months later. By doing this, a full supply of milk will be secured regularly throughout the year for years. When the first cow is half through her time of milking, the second one will come in; by the time the first one stops milking the third one will come in, and by the time the second one stops and the third one is half through her time, the first will calve again; and when the third one stops and the first is half through, the second will calve again, and so on. But this presupposes proper care and management, otherwise all three cows may stop milking together.

If a very large supply of milk be wanted, and a large number of cows has to be kept, and it is not practicable to keep them when they run dry, then cows in full milk should be bought, and before they run quite dry they should be sold and replaced by others that have newly calved. This plan may suit some dairymen, whose only object is to make as much money in as short a time as possible, but is not the wisest or best plan for the family to pursue. For the family, as well as good dairy-farmers, the first plan is the cheapest and safest.

Good cows are not easily procured, and when a person has one, he ought to keep her. She will amply repay him; besides, it is not only a great pity, but a decided loss to the country, and very wrong to sell good cows to butchers.

If anyone has really good cows in calf that they wish to sell, they ought to advertise them. Many European and native gentlemen would be only too glad to buy them, and would pay better prices than the butchers usually give.

Servants' Tricks.—Now, the next thing to do before purchasing the cow is, not to allow your servants to have a hand in the purchasing. All servants, from the sirdar bearer down to the mehter, will conspire to prevent their master from profiting by the possession of cows. The khansama would much rather that milk and butter be bought, as he not only takes a percentage —*dustoori*—on all bills, but also levies a fee upon the milkman for his khansamaship's patronage. The bearer must have his commission from the man who sells the cow to his master, and the man who will give the largest commission is sure to get the preference; and though the cow be an inferior or diseased one, he will pronounce it perfectly good, and persuade his master to buy it, and will prevent other and better cows being brought to his master. Thus, the oftener cows have to be sold and new ones bought, the greater is his gain. The cook also prefers to buy the butter and ghee for the use of the kitchen, and put down six *chittacks* in his account when he has only used four. A careful housekeeper will measure the milk and butter, and thus make herself disagreeable in more ways than one; so, as a rule, all table servants and cooks set themselves against their masters keeping cows, and if they have a hand in the matter they will do all they can to make the cows failures. If the bearer or any other servant is allowed a hand in the purchase of the cows or in their feed and keep, he will be sure to make them at least an expensive luxury.

On account of servants' tricks it is almost impossible to get any article of food in India in its original purity. In order to give *dustoori* the sellers are obliged to adulterate the things, otherwise where would be their gain? One reason why gowallahs water their milk, and otherwise adulterate it is, they have to make up for the heavy commissions they have to pay. If a milkman is honest and will not adulterate his milk, and refuses to pay *dustoori*, he soon finds his milk is condemned and rejected, and he loses his customer. The servants can so easily spoil the milk and blame the milkman for giving bad milk, that it is impossible for any milkman to be honest so long as the servants are allowed to meddle with him and the milk. I blame the masters and mistresses for the continuance of this evil practice. I never allow my servants to take *dustoori* from any person, consequently I am not troubled much by them.

Native gentlemen suffer very much from the dishonesty of their servants, dependants, and even relatives. Before a man can sell anything to a Raja or Baboo, he has to bribe the servants and hangers-on, from the son-in-law down to the piak or syce. In order to do this the seller has to increase the price of his goods; thus the Baboo has to pay his dishonest relatives and servants for the privilege of buying even a cow or a donkey.

In keeping cows, comfort to the family must be combined with profit to the purse.

Buying a Cow with a Calf.—If a cow that has calved be purchased, she should be brought to the buyer's house immediately after calving, and kept under proper treatment until the calf is three weeks old. Bad management at such a time will permanently spoil a cow. A cow is not in full milk until the twenty-first day after calving, and during this period she is liable to many ailments.

Buying a Cow in Calf.—If a dry cow be purchased, she should be bought at least a fortnight before her time for calving, so that she might get used to her new house and attendant. If the cow be one that the intending purchaser knows, or if she be recommended by a trustworthy person who really knows something about cows, then it is well to buy her before she has calved, otherwise the risk of being cheated is great.

There are many advantages in buying dry cows (see Chapter XII.), but one has to be careful.

If the intending purchaser be not a good judge of cattle, he ought to get the help of someone who is, even if he has to pay him for his services.

CHAPTER IV.

POINTS IN A GOOD COW.

Outward Appearance.—A good cow is loose-limbed and has a large body; her head is small and her forehead broad; her coat is soft and silky, and her tail thin and flexible, with a rich and glossy (often wavy) bunch of hair at the end; her horns point backward, not forward, though occasionally a good cow with horns pointing forward is met with; she has short legs, wide hips, and a deep, broad chest, and is long barrelled; her hams are wide apart, as if nature had intended her to have a large udder when in milk. In a heifer the milk-vein is not visible, but when a cow is about to calve, if she is going to be a good milker, it will be very apparent, and will have the appearance of a cord stretching along the lower part of her stomach; her teats will be well developed and large.

The limbs of a good cow are loose and large, and the flesh on them rather hangs downwards. A fat, sleek cow is probably a gross feeder, and what she eats runs into fat.

Neatly built heifers, with nicely rounded limbs and a tendency to fat rumps (not hams), usually do not prove to be good cows.

Temper.—A good cow is slow and lazy in her movements, and looks motherly. Brisk, frisky cows are seldom good milkers, and very often are vicious and troublesome at milking time. A good milker is of a dull, quiet temperament, and only becomes excited when her calf is frightened or touched by a stranger. Some are so good-tempered that they will allow even strangers to touch them and their calves, without getting in the least excited. A cow with her first calf is more excitable than an older one.

Colour.—Black, dark brown, and red cows are generally healthy and strong. The milk of a red cow is the sweetest. Red cows, generally, have good digestions. A greyish white is a very common colour in India; a cow of this colour at some seasons will be quite white, and at others a dark grey. This colour is not confined to any special breed, but as a rule such cows are not good milkers. When the grey takes the form of piebald the cow will probably prove a very good one. A creamy white denotes richness of blood, and if at the same time the inside of the ears and the hoofs be a bright yellow, the milk will be very rich and produce a large quantity of butter; and if the hair be also fine, the cow will, in all probability, prove a large milker as well as a rich one.

The milk of a pearly or bluish white cow, with little or no yellow in her skin, will be poor and bluish.

Quality of Milk.—"Every cow gives milk of a different quality and colour. When selecting a cow, the quality and colour (as well as the quantity) of her milk must be taken into consideration. If the cow is in milk, take a little of her milk in a clear wineglass and examine it. If the milk be of a bluish hue it is poor. There is generally a good deal of *serum* in the milk of cows that are very large milkers, and such milk does not produce much cream or butter, but it is exceedingly good for young children. The yellower the milk the better: therefore a cow giving yellow milk is more valuable than one giving bluish milk. Many cows that give rich yellow milk make up in quality what they lack in quantity. Cows giving a very large quantity of milk are exceedingly delicate, as all their strength runs into milk, and sometimes they leave off calving earlier than they should. A cow that gives from eight to ten *seers* of milk a day is a first-rate one for all practical purposes." —*Cows in India.*

Blind Nipples.—Some cows of the best milking breeds have this blemish. Blind nipples show a tendency to gathering in the udder, which is very troublesome, and often renders a cow quite useless. Cows with blind nipples should be avoided. The four nipples should be of the same length and at equal distances apart.

Scarred Cows.—Because a cow happens to be scarred about the face, neck, or shoulders, it is no reason that she must be rejected. Natives fire and brand their cows for some of the simplest ailments, and these scars may be the results of severe treatment of some such disease. But a cow should always be thoroughly examined to see if she is suffering from any disease.

Age.—When buying a cow it is best to select a young one, although an older cow will give more and richer milk. A young cow will always sell well after she has milked for six or eight years, while an old cow may soon fail to calve or suddenly stop her milk, and thus become worthless. Again, an old cow is subject to many difficulties in calving from which the younger one is exempt. A cow about to have her second calf is a good one to choose, as she has got over the difficulties of her first calving, and will give her full supply of milk.

" It costs more to make milk from old cows than it does from young ones having the same milk-producing capacity. The period of profitable milking does not terminate at the same age with all cows alike. Some hold out longer than others, but as a rule the best efforts do not reach beyond the eighth year of the cow's age. The quantity of milk given generally keeps up until a cow is ten years old, and sometimes considerably longer; but after a cow has reached her eighth year, her milk is produced at a greater cost of feed, and after that age it costs more to fatten her, while her flesh depreciates in quality."—*American Farmer.*

Number of Calves a Cow has had.—" The value of a cow depends so much on the number of calves she has had, that no reliance can be placed on the statement of sellers on this point, and the buyer must trust to his own judgment.

" The best way of judging is by the figure. The hips become more prominent, the belly lower, the skinny parts of the body lengthen and hang, and the udder becomes more raggy after each calf. A cow carrying her first calf shows her condition but little, but an old one decidedly so; with a little experience it is not difficult to determine about how many times a cow has calved.

" It is impossible to tell how often a cow will calve: some have been known to produce as many as twenty, and some have not given more than five. Eight is the average number; after the eighth calf a cow is supposed to be of no market value, although she may have two or three more calves."—*Cows in India.*

A Good Milker.—If the cow brought for sale be in milk, have her milked in your presence. Even if she be nearly dry, it will be easy to judge by the breadth of the stream whether she is a good milker or not. A broad stream shows a good milker, and a thin, poor stream a scanty milker. When a good milker is milked, the milk will rattle against the vessel with a steady rush: anyone who has seen cows milked will easily recognise this particular sound; when the supply is scanty the milk passages are crude and small, and the milk cannot flow freely.

A good milker will give all her milk at one drawing, but a poor milker will need to have the calf mouth her two or three times before all the milk can be extracted.

A Slinker.—If a cow has once slipped her calf, she is very liable to do it again, and it is not safe to buy her when in calf. Slinking very often is hereditary.

If a cow has calved much before her full time it is liable to affect the quantity of her milk.

If the calf has died after its birth, the mother's milk will rapidly decrease.

Calves.—When purchasing a cow be particular that the calf is as well-bred as its mother. The calf's breed will affect the mother's supply of milk as well as its own value. (See Chapter XIV.)

CHAPTER V.

FOOD.

Proper Care and Treatment of Milking Cows.—Cows are delicate creatures, and their supply of milk greatly depends upon the management and care they receive. Naturally this supply is only sufficient to feed the calf, but under proper care and management it largely exceeds this amount. As a highly cultivated plant, when neglected, returns to its wild state, so cattle, if not properly cared for, will soon deteriorate, and the milk of the cow will greatly diminish and sometimes altogether stop. Proper care and treatment are essential to keep up the unnaturally large supply of milk.

It is very easy to spoil a cow, and if owners do not exercise unremitting vigilance it will be impossible to keep their cows in full milk, and their bulls and bullocks in working order. In addition to vigilance, they must know something about the treatment of cattle both in health and sickness, when in milk or when dry.

Food.—The cow's food is one of the things that needs

the most careful attention. Cows are clean and fastidious feeders, and every cow will not eat the same kind of food. The feeding utensils must be kept perfectly clean and free from any disagreeable smell, or else the cow will not eat her food. If anything offensive have chanced to get into the food the cow will refuse the whole of it; sometimes it happens that a little piece of dung will get into the straw or *bhoosa*, or in the oilcake, and the whole of the food will be wasted. The water that the food is mixed with must be perfectly clean. Bad food or water will seriously affect the milk.

Some food should always be given to the cow immediately before she is milked, as the rush of milk on an empty stomach tries her strength. If half a *seer* of bran is sprinkled over the food that remains in the feeding-trough in the morning it is all that is necessary.

After the cow has been milked in the morning she should be let out to graze until eight o'clock, then she must be brought in and given her regular morning meal.

It is not wise to keep the cow tied up in her stall all through the day and night. If she is not allowed sufficient exercise she will not keep in good health. The cow should be sent out to graze at all seasons (except when it rains heavily) for two or three hours in the morning. At eight o'clock she should be given her food and kept tied up for the rest of the day; cows like to be left alone quiet, with their food to eat at pleasure. She must be well supplied with good drinking water.

She should have her evening food at six o'clock. Sometimes it is best to give the food in three or four meals instead of two. Some cows will waste a great deal of food if much be given at one time, as the food begins to smell sour in a few hours.

Regularity in feeding must be strictly observed.

The Kinds of Grain that are Good for Cows.—Kullie or *woorid*, barley, and wheat, are the only kinds of grain that should be given to milk-cows; all other grains are more or less injurious. Rice is good for sick cattle, but has not much nutriment. Indian corn fattens, but does not increase milk. Indian corn bran is better. Khassari should never be given to cattle, goats or sheep. It is very heating and dries up the milk, and is also very indigestible and stunts the growth. It often produces paralysis. Gram should be given to only weak cows, and then not more than half a *seer* a day.

Quantity of Food.—The following should be divided into two or more meals in twenty-four hours, and is sufficient for a milk-cow of ordinary size giving eight *seers* of milk, but in the case of a large cow or a large milker the quantity should be proportionately increased. Small cows giving four or five *seers* of milk will not need so much.

Kullie (*woorid*), barley, or wheat	1½ seer
Bran (*bhoosi*), wheat, peas, kullie or rhurhur bran	2 seers
Oilcake (*khully*)	1 seer
Cotton-seed (*bunaula*), or gram	½ seer
Chaff (*bhoosa*), wheat, barley, kullie or mussoor chaff	3 seers
Green grass, chopped fine	12 seers
Salt	1 chittack
Sulphur	¼ chittack
Total	20 seers, 1¼ chittack

If the cow does not thrive on the above-mentioned quantity of food, give in addition from two to eight *seers* of chaff or straw.

When cotton-seed is not procurable, half a *seer* of gram should be given. When green grass cannot be procured, give extra chaff. If chaff (*bhoosa*) is not in stock, give paddy-straw and an extra *seer* of bran (*bhoosi*). Green grass is very essential to health, but during May and June it is very difficult to get any. In the place of grass give extra chaff, hay, or paddy-straw; give as much as the cow will eat.

The water in which rice has been washed, and the rice-*kanji* or *mar*, are very good for cows.

The quality of the food must be the best; it is no economy to feed cows upon damaged grain and bran, or rotten oilcake and straw.

Effects of the Different Kinds of Food.—Of the three

kinds of grain mentioned above as being the only ones that should be given to cows, kullie (*woorid*) is the best for milk-cows, as it produces milk as well as strengthens. But it is best to mix kullie, barley, and wheat in equal parts, as kullie is cooling, and some cows suffer a great deal from cold in the winter. Gram is the best for calves, bulls, and bullocks.

If the cow is not strong and is out of condition, the quantity of grain should be increased. Grain is nourishing.

If the cow's digestion is not good, the grain should be decreased and the wheat-bran increased.

If she is a small eater, the chaff and straw should be lessened, otherwise she will lose much of her food.

Green grass gives colour and richness to the milk and butter.

Grain increases the quantity and improves the quality of milk, and strengthens the cow.

Cotton-seed produces rich butter, but more than half a *seer* a day should never be given to any cow, as it is very heating and difficult to digest, and often causes inflammation of the udder.

Oilcake helps to produce milk and butter.

Bran helps digestion and produces milk.

Salt and sulphur are purifiers, and keep the bowels in proper condition, acting as preventives against many diseases.

There is no nourishment in paddy-straw; wheat, barley, and kullie *bhoosa* are much better.

All oilcakes are not good for milk-cows. The best are those made from *till* or *ulsee*, the *teesi* (linseed), and the cocoanut. Other kinds of oilcake are very heating, and therefore injurious to cows. The oilcake made from the mustard- or rye-seed is good for bullocks and bulls.

The *till* khully is sweet in flavour; it has an oily smell, and is of a chocolate colour, and if old is hard and dry. This is certainly *the* best for cows, but is rather difficult to procure; even if it costs more than the other kinds, it should be used in preference to any other. Next to the *till* and *teesi* in point of excellence is the cocoanut oilcake; cows generally do not like it at first, and it should be given fresh and in small quantities until they become accustomed to it. The mustard oilcake is the most common, and generally used by the natives; but is not suitable for milk-cows and young calves.

All these oilcakes form good nourishing food, and are invaluable for the formation of the various tissues that enter into the formation of the animal structure, to enrich the blood and promote secretion of milk. Great care should be taken that the oilcake is fresh and has no worms in it. The *till* oilcake, especially, soon goes bad and gets full of worms.

Preparation of Food.—The grain should always be ground and well boiled, and allowed to cool. Four or five *seers* of water should be added to every *seer* of grain, and then boiled; or else it should be allowed to soak for twelve hours after it has been well ground. Kullie should never be boiled; it should be ground fine and soaked for twelve hours. When kullie is boiled it seems to disagree with cattle.

The bran should be dry.

The cotton-seed should be thoroughly broken, and soaked until it gets quite soft.

The oilcake should be broken up into small pieces, and soaked for four hours, or else pounded up finely.

The chaff, grass, hay, or straw should be chopped fine —into pieces one inch in length.

The salt and sulphur should be ground and added to the grain when cool.

The whole should be well mixed up with a sufficient quantity of water or rice-*kanji* to make it sloppy.

Great care must be taken that the grain is not given whole and uncooked or unsoaked, and that the food is not given dry.

N.B.—Cows giving milk should never be allowed to grow very fat. When the food goes into fat the milk will decrease, and the cow become barren. In such cases the grain should be stopped in part or whole. But the cow must always be kept in good condition.

Cost of Food.—The cost of food varies in different parts of the country, and at different seasons of the year, but the food should never cost more than from half to three-fourths the value of the milk the cow gives.

Green Food.—Cows should never be deprived of green food; if they are, they will not keep in good health; besides, the milk will not be good.

The common villagers never think of giving their cattle any special food. The poor animals are let loose in the morning and tied up in the evening, and all the food they are allowed is what they manage to pick up in grazing, with the addition of perhaps a handful of dry paddy-straw at night.

Doob is the best grass for cattle. Young wheat, barley, kullie, peas, Indian corn stalks, and paddy, in their green and tender state, and green tender leaves of fruit trees, are excellent for cattle. The long juicy grass that grows among the Indian corn, wheat, and other crops makes splendid cattle fodder. Carrots chopped up, and sugar-cane and beetroot and, occasionally, cabbages, are very wholesome and good food.

Three and a half *biggahs* or one acre of land is what one cow needs to keep her supplied with green food throughout the year.

Straw.—Especial care should be exercised in the selection of the straw given to the cow. Wheat and barley straw are certainly the best that can be given to cattle. Wheat and barley straw are broken up and sold as *bhoosa* chaff. See that it is clean and sweet. Frequently it will be found full of mud, dung, leaves, and thorns, or be musty and rotten.

Paddy - straw has very little nourishment, but in Bengal it is the chief article of food for cattle. In selecting paddy-straw, be careful that it is not of paddy grown in swamps or low lands. Often such straw will make the cow sick. The straw of the finer quality of paddy grown on high lands is most suitable. Such straw will be nice and fine, of a clean light yellow colour, and will smell sweet and clean, but will be slightly saltish in taste.

Hay.—Cattle are not particularly fond of hay. Good, sweet, soft hay may be given in small quantities.

Filthy Food.—"In some parts of India cattle are fed on dreadful filth, horse-dung and stable litter, particularly that from artillery and cavalry stables, horse marts and other well-fed studs, where the animals receive much grain; not only this, but on night-soil also. The natives say it gives the milk a rich creamy look, and in no way affects the flavour. The poor cows are made to eat all this abomination by cruelty and starvation. And it has to be prepared and made palatable before they will touch it, but they soon learn to pick up all this stuff of their own accord." *Cows in India.*

Some cows die from the effects of bad feeding, and it is a wonder that more people do not die from drinking the milk of cows fed on filthy food.

Well-fed and properly cared-for cows will not eat anything filthy, and can be sent out to graze and exercise without the least fear of their picking up anything harmful to themselves or to their milk.

Salt.—If a cow does not get sufficient salt and a little sulphur in her food, she will pick up dry bones or lick earth.

Drink.—The cow's drinking-water must also be attended to. Pure water and a good supply of it is as absolutely necessary as good and sufficient food. Cows are very thirsty creatures, and if they do not get pure water they will drink whatever comes in their way

"In these days a great deal is said about village milk from badly fed cows producing typhoid fever; it is also asserted that dirty water is often mixed with bazaar milk; but if more attention were paid to the water cows drink I think the doctors would be nearer the mark. We all know to what filthy uses natives put jheels and ponds, and water from such places must be unfit for cows to drink, and will affect the milk just as much as filthy food."—*Cows in India.*

But what when such water is added to the milk?

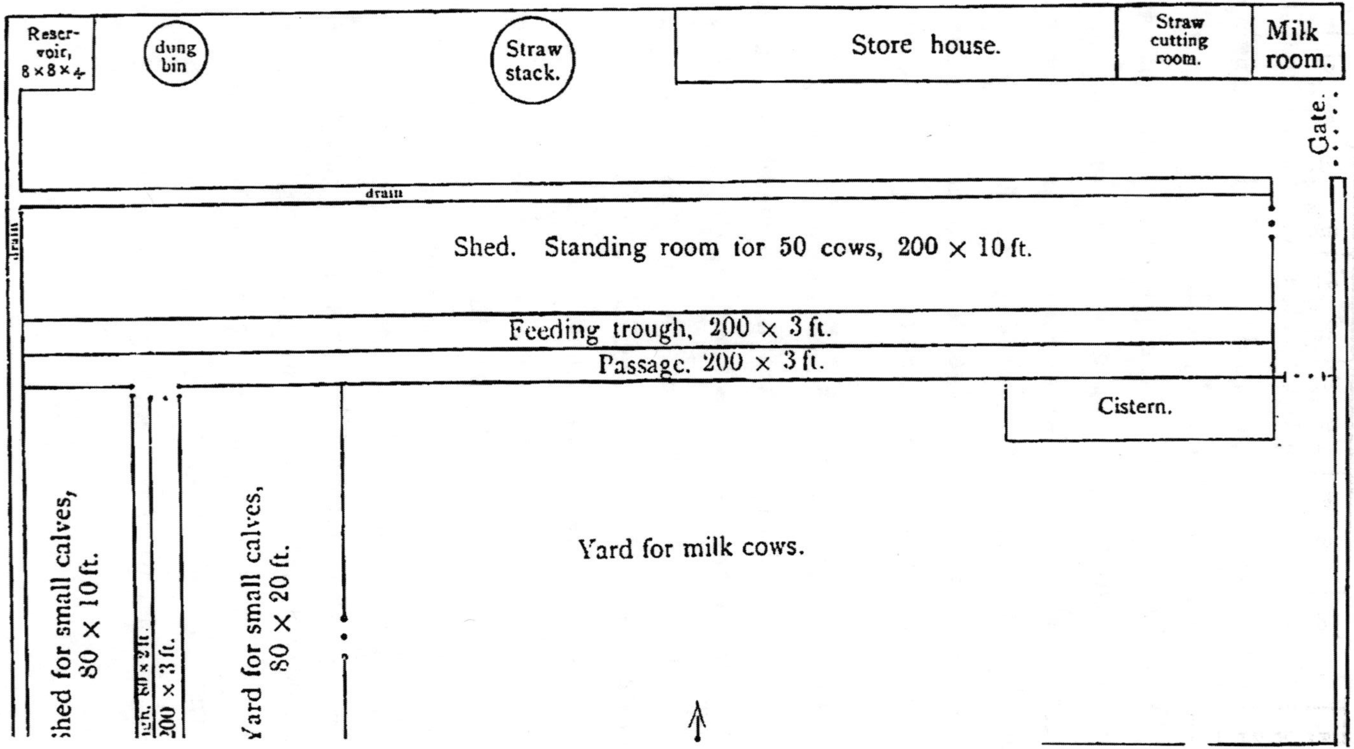
Reser-
voir,
8 × 8 × 4
dung
bin
Straw
stack.
Store house.
Straw
cutting
room.
Milk
room.
Gate.
drain
drain
Shed. Standing room for 50 cows, 200 × 10 ft.
Feeding trough, 200 × 3 ft.
Passage. 200 × 3 ft.
Cistern.
Yard for milk cows.
hed for small calves,
80 × 10 ft.
200 × 3 ft.
Yard for small calves,
80 × 20 ft.

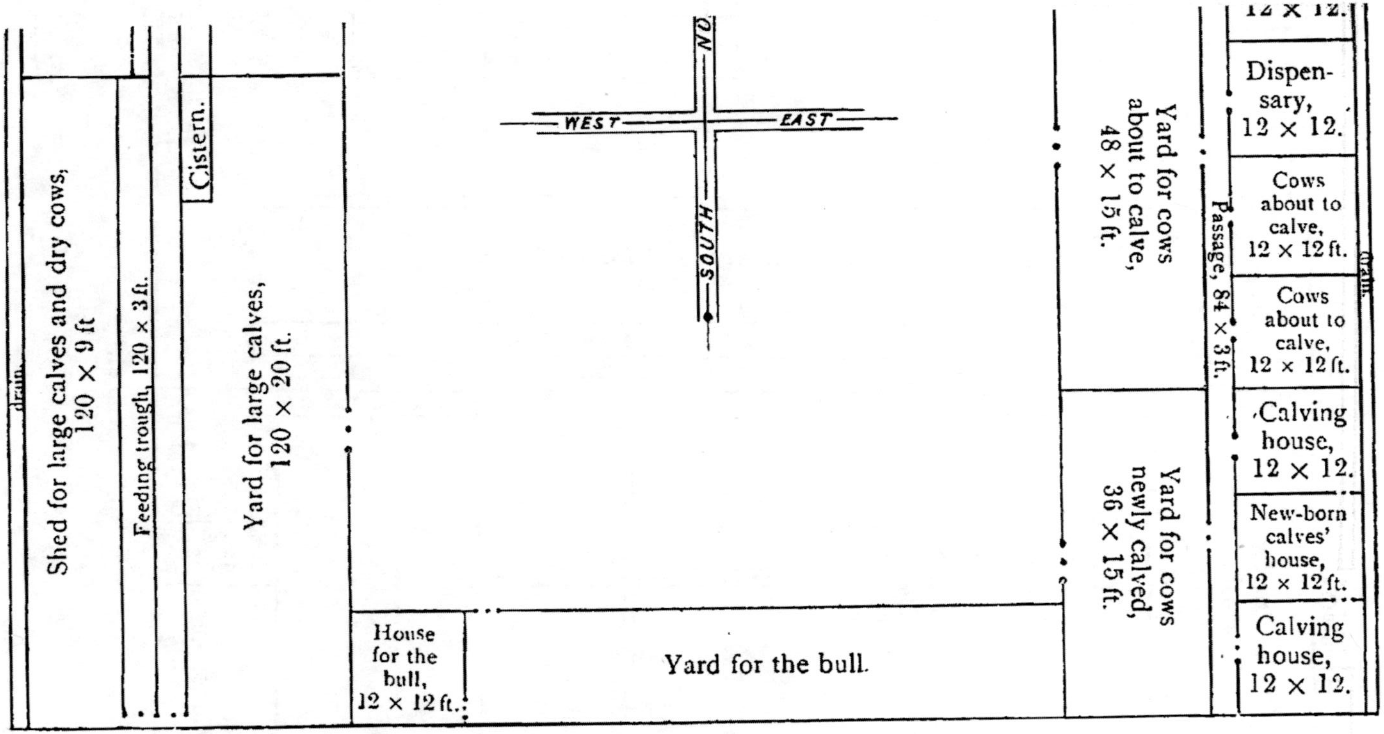

FIG. 20.—MODEL INDIAN DAIRY.

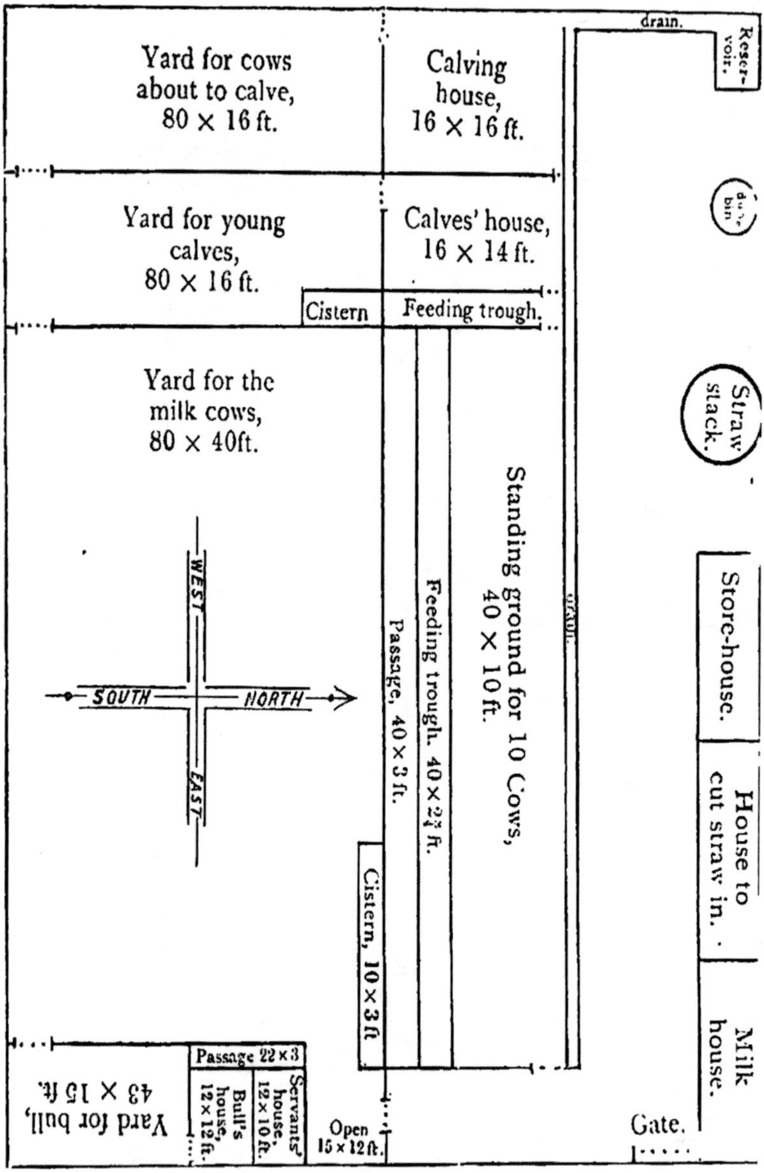
drain.
Reservoir.
Yard for cows about to calve, 80 × 16 ft.
Calving house, 16 × 16 ft.
Yard for young calves, 80 × 16 ft.
Calves' house, 16 × 14 ft.
Cistern
Feeding trough.
Straw stack.
Yard for the milk cows, 80 × 40ft.
WEST
SOUTH
NORTH
EAST
Standing ground for 10 Cows, 40 × 10 ft.
Feeding trough. 40 × 2½ ft.
Passage, 40 × 3 ft.
Store-house.
House to cut straw in.
Cistern, 10 × 3 ft.
Milk house.
Passage 22 × 3
Yard for bull, 43 × 15 ft.
Bull's house, 12 × 12 ft.
Servants' house, 12 × 10 ft.
Open 15 × 12 ft.
Gate.

Fig. 21.

CHAPTER VI.

HOUSE AND UTENSILS.

THE *cow-house* is a very important consideration. Cattle must be properly housed at nights, and sheltered from the midday sun, and from rain and storms.

In the cold weather their house must be free from draughts. In the rains it must be kept perfectly dry. In the hot weather it must be kept open and cool, and at all seasons it must be thoroughly ventilated.

It is not at all difficult to build a suitable house for cattle in India. A *pucca* house is preferable to a *kutcha* one, but a very nice one can be built of wooden posts or mud pillars and thatched roof, at a very small cost. Be the house *kutcha* or *pucca*, the floor must be of brick and cement. Mud floors soon wear into holes and become very offensive. Floors made of planks are very dangerous, as cattle slip on them, and are sometimes seriously injured. The best way to make the floor is to put down a lot of broken bricks (*khoa*) and lime, and beat down well; then over this put first-class bricks on edge, well pointed with cement. This flooring will last for years.

The level of the floor should be a foot and a half to two feet higher than the surrounding ground.

There are of course many ways of making a cow-house. If only one or two cows are kept, a room or

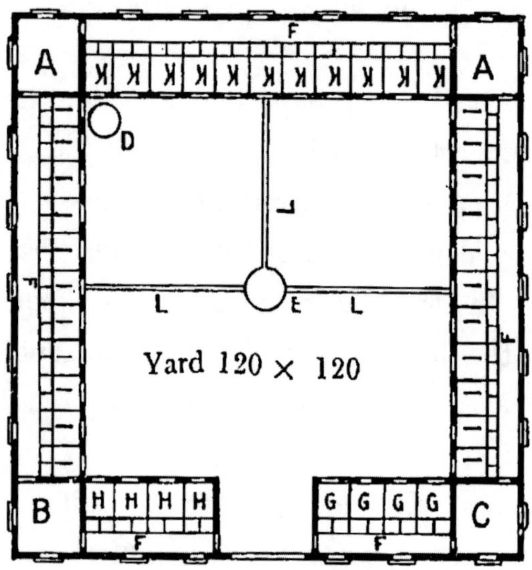

MODEL ENGLISH DAIRY.

FIG. 22.—A, storerooms; B, food preparing room; C, milk room; D, water cistern; E, reservoir; F, feeding passages; G, stalls for calves; H, stalls for calving and newly calved cows; I, stalls for milk-cows; K, stalls for dry cows and bull; L, drains.

two in the outhouses may be appropriated for them, or a stall or two in the stables be given up for their accommodation, but if many cows be kept, a regular cow-house must be built. Whatever the number of the cows, particular attention must be paid to the floor and ventilation.

I here give a plan of the kind of house I like best for cattle. Fig 21.

This is a very simple construction, and can be made as small or as large as necessary. It is divided into three compartments or houses: one for the cows to calve in, one for the calves when away from their

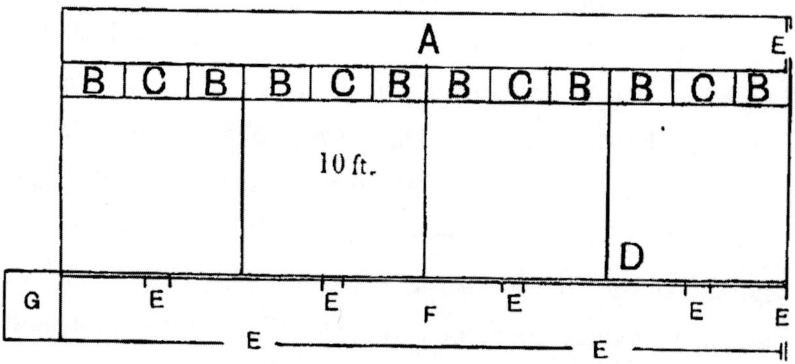

FIG. 23.—Stalls for cows, two in each stall. A, passage; B, feeding trough; C, water trough; D, calves' room; E, doors; F, verandah to prepare food; G, reservoir; H, drain.

mothers, and one for the larger cattle. The house or houses should always open to the south. The north side must be walled up and have small windows (about 3 feet by 2 feet) 5 feet above the ground and 6 feet apart. The width of the house inside should be at least 16 feet. From the north wall there should be 10 feet of standing ground, then 3 feet occupied by the feeding trough, and lastly, 3 feet for a passage behind the trough. The feeding trough to be made of brick and cement running the whole length of the room. The inside of the trough should be from 18 to 21 inches wide, and 12 to 15 inches deep, but the bottom should be raised at least 12 inches from the level of the floor, making it in all from 24 to 27 inches high. The floor of the house should slope off from south to north—that is, from the head of the cow to her hind quarters. The slope should not exceed 3 inches—just sufficient to carry off all the urine. Right against the north wall there should be a drain to receive and carry off all the droppings. This drain should be 6 or 9 inches wide, and 3 inches deep, made of bricks and cement. Outside the cow-house, 8 feet from it to the north, there should be a reservoir 4 feet by 4 feet and 2 feet deep to receive all the urine and water, and the drain of the cow-house should connect with this reservoir.

The roof on the south should be supported by pillars made of either brick, mud, or wood. If made of bricks, each pillar should be 24 inches by 15 inches, if of mud, it should be 36 inches by 18 inches, and the opening or doorway between each pillar should not be less than 6 feet wide.

The calving or calves' rooms or houses should be the same as the cows' house, only, for the calves the feeding trough should be not more than a foot wide, and 6 to

9 inches deep inside; the whole of the trough should not be more than 15 inches high.

Ventilation in this house will be perfect, and it will not be at all difficult to keep the floor perfectly clean and dry at all seasons. During the warm weather, the doors and windows should be kept entirely open during the day and at night; in the cold weather and in rain-storms, the north windows should be kept closed day and night, but the doors should be open during the day, and closed at night. The top part of the doors should have ventilators large enough to admit of sufficient ventilation when the doors are closed.

The doors and windows can be made of mats or wood; the latter is preferable. Purdahs of good stout canvas or tarpaulin also answer well.

The height of the house or room should not be less than 10 feet from floor to ceiling; the doorways should be 8 feet high. If the house be thatched or tiled, the sides should be at least 8 feet, and the centre 12 feet high.

Space.—Cattle should never be crowded up together. Ample room should be given them to not only stand, but also to sit and lie down comfortably. No cow will keep in good health unless she has 40 feet of standing ground—10 feet by 4 feet. If the cows be large ones, it will be well to allow them each 60 feet of ground—10 feet by 6 feet. For a single cow a room at least

10 feet by 8 feet is necessary, giving her sufficient room to comfortably turn round.

Keeping the Floor Clean and dry is an indispensable necessity. It must not only be swept clean every morning and evening, but must be thoroughly scrubbed and washed every morning, and swept every time it is soiled. The droppings must not be allowed to remain on the floor or in the drain any length of time. The house must be kept clean and sweet and perfectly dry. Phenyle and water or carbolic powder should be sprinkled on the floor every day. Throwing sand on the floor, or putting down some straw, will prevent the cattle from slipping on the *pucca* floor. The cows should be allowed some dry straw to lie on in the cold weather and rains. Especial attention must be given to the calves' house and the calving house.

The best time to wash the house is when the cows are let out into the yard in the morning.

Drains.—The drain of the cow-house must be connected with the public underground street sewer, or else with the reservoir behind the house, already spoken of. This reservoir must be emptied and washed every day, and the contents either buried deep underground, or else removed far from the cow-house. The dung should be gathered and kept in a bin at the back of the cow-shed until it is removed in the morning.

Utensils.—If only one or two cows be kept, zinc or

galvanised tubs (not iron) can be used for them. I do not recommend wooden or earthen tubs, as they never can be kept clean, whereas the zinc or galvanised ones can be thoroughly scrubbed and washed every morning and evening. If these tubs cannot be got, then earthen *gumlahs* (nads) should be put down as the natives do them; but great care is needed to prevent them from smelling offensively, and they should be frequently changed for new ones.

If a number of cattle be kept, the *pucca* cemented trough is the best to have. It will be a great saving in labour. It will take a man nearly half a day to clean a dozen tubs, whereas the trough for the same number of cows can be properly cleaned in half an hour. Besides, cattle eat with more comfort out of a raised trough than they do out of tubs.

When milk-cows and dry cows and bullocks are kept in the same room, the trough should be divided into two or three divisions, for the same food will not be given to all. If possible, dry cows and bullocks should be kept in separate rooms or houses from milk-cows.

The tubs and trough must be thoroughly scrubbed and washed every morning and evening.

Cistern.—There should always be a cistern in every cow-house. The best position for it is immediately outside of the shed on the south in the yard (see sketch of cow-house). This cistern should always be kept filled with pure drinking-water. It should be properly cleaned and refilled every morning. When the cows are let out into the yard, they can have a good refreshing drink. Cattle should be watered at least twice a day.

Mode of Tying.—If only one or two cows be kept, they should be tied to separate pegs far apart, that they may not reach each other; but when a number are feeding at the trough, they must be so tied that they will not reach one another. The best mode of tying them is this: put down thick iron rods as posts 4 feet apart all along the trough: to these posts tie good stout pieces of rope.

Each rope is 6 feet long, and is tied by the two ends to two posts, one on either side; to the centre of this rope another rope about 4 feet long is attached, which goes round the cow's neck, and so secures her that she cannot reach her neighbour to the right or left, but at the same time she has ample freedom to stand erect and to sit or lie down with comfort. The ropes should be tied to the top of the posts on a level with the top of the trough. A better plan would be to have iron rings round the posts, and tie the ropes to the rings. This would enable the animal to sit or rise with greater ease, as the ring will slide up or down the post as necessary.

Bullocks and large calves should be tied in the same manner as the cows, but bulls must be tied far apart with very strong ropes or chains, as they will do much damage if they happen to break loose.

The Yard.—Every cow-house should have a yard attached to it, in which milk-cows can be let loose for a couple of hours in the morning. This freedom and exercise are very necessary, and will be very beneficial to the animal's health. The yard should be in front of the cow-house. Each animal should have at least 400 feet of ground—40 feet by 10 feet—in the yard, but the more given the better. Dry cows, bullocks, and calves should be sent out to graze or kept loose in the yard during the day.

Other Houses.—The servants' houses and the storehouse should be detached from the cow-house, at least 50 feet from it, or else on the west of the house in the same line. There should also be a little room for keeping the milk utensils and receiving and measuring the milk. If possible, the bull's house should be detached from the main building, and should have a separate yard (as in Fig. 20 and 21).

A good study of the ground plan of the cow-sheds herein given, will clearly show the reader what is necessary in such an establishment.

FIG. 24.—COW-SHED.

CHAPTER VII.

ATTENDANTS.

In order to keep cows with any degree of success, it is necessary to have proper servants. A great many people buy cows, and engage gowallahs, and leave the poor animals to the tender mercies of these men, and are exceedingly surprised when they find in a few months that the cows are spoiled, or the calves have died. Others, again, put the cows in the care of the bearer or khansama, and cannot understand why the animals give so little milk, or why their food costs so much. So they conclude that keeping cows is a failure, and that Indian cows do not give much milk, and the calves never live. People must always remember that there is a right and a wrong way of doing a thing, and if a person goes the wrong way about it, he must expect failure. If one desires to derive any pleasure and profit from keeping cows, he must attend to them himself, having them under his immediate supervision. If the servants or any other person be entrusted with their sole management, the enterprise will end in failure and disappointment.

While one personally looks after the animals, he will need servants to do the work and carry out his instructions.

If only one cow be kept, the syce's wife or the wife of some other servant can well look after her, if she is paid one or two rupees a month. But if a number of cows be kept, it will be necessary to have servants specially for them. One man cannot take care of more than six cows, but it is best for him to have only four; if more be given him they will not be properly cared for.

The Servant's Disposition of Mind.—The temper of the cowherd has a great deal to do with the health and temper of the animals under his care. He must not only be clean and active, but must also have a love, or at least a liking, for the cows, and be kind and gentle to them. If he is harsh and rough, and drives them about, they will become excited and cross, will not eat their food properly, and will give trouble at milking. Cattle get thin and sickly under harsh treatment. A bad-tempered servant should never be kept under any consideration.

Servants' Fidelity.—Then again, the cowherd must be faithful, and not only an eye-server. True, such a man among Indian servants would be a prodigy, but the servants must be taught to be faithful to the animals under their care; otherwise, when the master and mistress happen to be away from home, or sick for a day or two, the cattle will suffer. It need never be expected that the servants will give the animals the same care and attention as the master or mistress will give, but they can be made to understand what is expected of them, and that they must do the work properly if they want to serve. It takes a long time, sometimes months, to get this idea properly instilled into their minds. If the servants see that the master and mistress are careful and watchful, it will make them more attentive.

Native servants imagine they know more about cattle than their masters do. In some cases, it is true, owners of cattle are more ignorant than their stupid servants. The prejudice and ignorance of the natives are hard to overcome. They are unwilling to do anything their grandfathers and great-grandfathers did not do. The custom of the country is law with them.

The Caste of the Servants.—I do not like the gowallahs. They are generally very troublesome, and I very seldom employ them. Among Hindoos, the gowallah is of all men the most cruel to cattle. He will neglect and starve them if allowed to. He imagines he has a divine right to the cow and all that belongs to her, and resents any interference with his ways and doings. Any other caste man, even a Mohammedan, will do for a cowherd.

The *Aheer* is a good man to have as a cowman. He makes a good servant when properly trained.

CHAPTER VIII.

WASHING, GROOMING, AND EXERCISE.

Washing.—Cattle should be kept perfectly clean. When in health they should be regularly washed, bathed once or twice a week in the hot weather, once a week or once a fortnight in the rains, and once a month in the cold season. A bright sunny day should be selected for washing. The animals must be thoroughly dried and let loose after the bath. Great care must be taken to prevent them from taking a chill. Milk-cows are very liable to chills. Calves under six months old should not be bathed.

Grooming.—Cattle should be properly groomed every day. The same kind of brush as used for the horse should be used for the cow. Proper and regular grooming will keep cattle in good condition, and will prevent their having lice and ticks. Little calves ought to be brushed and the ticks, etc., picked off every second day or so.

Exercise.—Cows need regular exercise; working bullocks have enough of it, but milch-cows and calves should be let out to graze and exercise for a few hours every day. It is a great mistake to keep them tied up all the time. Close confinement causes disease.

Dry cows, heifers, and large calves should be let out to graze the whole day. Bulls need lots of exercise too; they should be tied with a long stout rope—40 feet long—in the yard, or if there be an enclosed yard, let loose in it.

Protection.—Cattle need protection from the midday sun and heavy rains. If there are no large trees on the grounds, under the shade of which the cattle can stand, then they should be taken into the shed during the hottest hours of the day, and when it rains heavily, or when the winds are cold and damp.

CHAPTER IX.

BREEDING.

BREEDING one's own cows is the surest method of attaining success in the dairy. When a cow is bought you are not at all sure of her blood; she herself may be a large and rich milker, and may milk for a long time, but you are not sure of her producing the same qualities in her progeny. Her parents may not have been of a good milking strain, and though she herself is a good cow, her calves may not be half so good. It sometimes happens that inferior mothers produce very superior daughters, but this does not occur very often. The general rule is, that like produces like. An inferior cow should never be bred from. And I personally would not breed from a cow whose mother and father as well as grandparents were not as superior as herself. Very often cows as well as other animals throw back—that is, the young ones do not take after the mother and father, but after the grandparents.

Breeding one's own cows is very often cheaper than buying them. If one has extensive grass-lands, he will find it more economical to breed than to buy. But it will not pay in cities, where one has to pay heavily for every morsel the cows eat. Then again, in breeding one's own cattle one avoids contagion. Disease is often brought into a dairy through cows that have been purchased.

It is Cheaper to Breed one's own Cows.—The calf has to be kept ten months, or as long as the cow gives milk. If properly cared for and managed, the heifer will take the bull when she is two years and three months old, and yield her first calf when she is three years old. So one has to keep the animal for two years and two months after her mother stops milking and before she has her first calf. The cost of her keep and food for these twenty-six months will not exceed from Rs. 50 to Rs. 70. This is exactly half the value of a really good cow. If the heifer, when she calves, gives ten *seers* of milk a day, she will sell for at least Rs. 120—just double what she has cost for food and keep.

The art of breeding is governed by a few rules, which are simple and easy to understand; and these rules must be faithfully observed if any degree of success is to be gained.

The first and most important of these is, that "like produces like," by which is meant that animals of certain peculiarities of form, colour, disposition, habit, health, and quality, when bred together, reproduce their own characteristics in their progeny. This rule has been so uniformly and constantly proved by practice, and is so reasonable and natural, that it may be taken as a safe guide in rearing cows. Every person may see it proved by practice every day of his life. There is more or less of family likeness in the lower animals as well as in persons. The calf of a Hansi cow and Hansi bull is always a Hansi, and the same is true of all other breeds. Parents of rich milking strains produce calves that will be good milkers, and bear a close resemblance to themselves in all valuable points.

Generally cow-calves take after their fathers, and in breeding great care is needed in the selection of the bull. The bull should always be superior to the cow, and must be of a good milking strain. Both the bull and cow should be the best specimen of their breed. (See Chapter X.)

1st. Never use an inferior bull.

2nd. Never breed from an inferior cow.

3rd. To improve the breed, the cow must be crossed by a bull that is superior to her. If the bull be inferior to the cow, the calf will be inferior to the mother; but if the bull be superior to the cow, the calf will be superior to the mother.

4th. Never breed in — that is, never breed from a father and daughter, or from a mother and son, neither from brothers and sisters. If close relations be bred from, the progeny will deteriorate.

5th. To breed successfully, proper food and careful management are necessary.

An experienced dairyman and large breeder writes thus—

"The calves are the means for the improvement of the dairy. By a gradual course of breeding, rearing, and development, the calves become the basis for all the skill of the dairyman's work in improving his stock, and in increasing their valuable product. Breed is made up of food and the most skilful care; and by judicious management the calves are developed into more useful and productive animals than their dams, until in course of time the improvement becomes fixed, and is inherited by the progeny. It is in this way that the improved breeds have been made up.

"The feeding of a heifer should be liberal. She should have regular rations of the food prepared and given to the cows, and about half as much of it will be eaten profitably. Liberal feeding of good food develops the digestive functions, and the training of a heifer for the dairy should be such as to encourage the healthful disposal of as much food as possible. It does not matter if the heifer should get fat, if the growth is not stunted by it. The gradual development of the normal figure of the model cow should be watched, and as long as this development is going on satisfactorily the feeding may be persevered in. Excessive fatness, however, is a bar to usefulness in the dairy, and when heifers with this tendency to fat come in, there is usually some defect which spoils the animal for a cow.

"Breed is undoubtedly dependent upon food. Feeding and training have given the value to the breed, and this value must be kept up by feeding and training. The mistake is often made of getting a pure-bred animal, and subjecting it to all the careless management which is given to the common stock, and expecting that this animal, by virtue of its parents' character, can lift up the common herd, and double or treble its value in a few years. Such a hope is doomed to disappointment from the outset. When a pure animal is brought into a herd, its care should be at least equal to that which it has been used to, and the very same system of feeding and general management should be followed with the whole herd. If this practice is followed, success will be sure, and the desired end will be reached.

"The training of heifers for their duties in the dairy should be a constant care of the dairyman. Vicious animals, which kick, hold up their milk, suck themselves, and practise the other usual vices of disorderly cows, are all made so by want of, or misdirected, training. The first lesson the calf learns should be affection for its owner, fearlessness and docility. Having never been maltreated it has no sense of fear, and accepts the attention of its owner without alarm. Receiving nothing but kindness and its food from him, it is always ready to meet him with eagerness, and soon learns to come at his call. Its natural instincts are even readily controllable, because its acquired docility accustoms it to give way to the management of its owner, and it never practises those vices which are intolerable in a dairy. It becomes in every respect a domesticated animal; and to attain this result, with all the comfort and advantages it involves, should be the constant care of the dairyman whose crop of calves is being harvested. Kindliness and gentleness in the owner are indispensable to these virtues in his cattle."—*H. Stewart.*

I shall say more upon this head in the chapter upon Calves and their Management.

CHAPTER X.

BULLS.

The Necessity for a Bull.—When there are a number of cows in the dairy, it will be necessary also to keep a good bull to breed from. If there are only one or two cows, and there is a good bull in the neighbourhood, the cows can be sent out when they come into season. The charge will not be much. In Northern India there are Government bulls at different stations kept for the benefit of the public, and anyone can have their services for the asking. But if there is no good bull in the neighbourhood, one must be got without delay; for it will never do to have good cows served by inferior bulls.

Every dairy-farm should have one or two first-class bulls. Unless the cows are put to the bull at the proper time, they will be spoiled for all future dairy use.

It is a great loss to have a cow served by an inferior bull. If a cow is served by a good bull, her milk will increase, but it will be sure to decrease if served by an inferior one. Some good cows are thus spoiled. Then again, the calf from an inferior bull will be inferior, and will sell for little or nothing.

Whatever breed is selected, great care must be taken that he is of the best type of that breed. The thoroughbred Hansi, Nellore, or Guzerati bulls are the best to breed from.

Indian Bulls versus *English Bulls.*—It is a mistake to cross Indian cows by English bulls; the progeny rapidly deteriorate. A cross between the best Indian bull and a Shorthorn cow will prove more satisfactory. If English blood is desired, I would advocate the following plan. Cross a good Shorthorn, Suffolk, or Jersey cow with a first-class bull of the best milking strain of one of the following breeds:—Hissar, Nellore, or Guzerati. I prefer the Hissar. Select a good bull-calf from this cross, and when he is three years old, use him for covering the Hissar cows or the cows of the breed his father was. This method will produce large strong calves that will prove superior milkers. The half-bred English and Hissar heifer should be covered by a pure-bred Hissar bull.

Points in a Good Bull.—The height of the bull will depend on his breed. But the larger he is the better. He must be deep and wide in the chest, long and broad in the back, and round in the barrel, well ribbed up and strong in the shoulders and limbs, and have massive but not very long legs; large joints, and legs fairly apart to support the body; compact and solid-looking carcases; short face, with large, prominent eyes, set far apart, and broad forehead and muzzle. His neck must be short and stout, rising well over the withers into a large hump. The head should be carried erect. The dew-lap should be long, but the ears should not be very long.

Age.—It is a very serious mistake to use an immature bull for breeding purposes. The progeny of such a bull will be weak and very hard to rear, and very often the mother's milk will decrease very perceptibly. A bull should never be used before he is three years old, and after he is eight years old. Some bulls are used when they are only two years of age, but this is a very bad practice. Very often very young or inferior bulls prove unproductive.

Care and Attention.—A bull needs proper care and attention. Some people let him loose to wander about at pleasure, and pick up what he can in the way of food, and never think of giving him any shelter or special attention. If the bull is not looked after he will be spoiled. He must be sheltered at nights and from the midday sun and heavy rains, and must have good wholesome food regularly.

Food.—Feed him twice a day, once at 8 A.M. and

again at sunset. The following is sufficient for two meals for a large Hansi bull:—

Oilcake (*khully*)	2 seers
Bran (*bhoosi*)	2 seers
Green grass	4 seers
Chaff (*bhoosa*)	4 seers
Salt	1 chittack
Sulphur	½ chittack

Besides this, 20 bundles of straw, or 15 bundles of hay, or 20 *seers* of green grass, must be given him in every twenty-four hours. Wherever it is possible, the bull should be tied out to graze. When this is done, and if there be sufficient grass on the land, the straw, hay, or extra green grass need not be given him.

Utensils, House and Grooming.—The feeding utensils and the house should be kept scrupulously clean, and the animal regularly groomed and washed, and allowed plenty of exercise. It is not at all a bad plan to give him some light work every day, such as drawing water or working the cart to remove the refuse, but he must not be in the least tired out. This will keep him docile.

Fat.—A bull should never be allowed to become very fat, but should always be in good condition.

Keeping him Separate.—Some people allow the bull to run with the cows in the herd. If the bull be a large one and very quiet, this may be done without harm, but most bulls are best kept apart, and should be allowed the company of the cow only when she needs his services.

Serving.—When a cow is in heat she should be tied up and the bull put to her. One or two servings are enough. This will conserve the bull's strength, which is wasted when he is allowed to run after the cow, or the cow is allowed to jump about.

Over-serving.—Bulls are generally spoiled by over-serving. A bull should not be allowed to serve more than two cows a week. An occasional deviation from this rule will not hurt him if he is allowed to serve each cow only once or twice. If a bull be used too much, he will become barren, or else the calves from him will be weak, and die early. This is one of the chief defects in *bazaar bulls* and Government bulls kept for serving the cows of the public.

Jail Dairies.—Most of the jails have fairly good cows, but very inferior bulls. Instead of keeping superior Hissar, Nellore, or Guzerati bulls, they have third-rate cross-breds or miserable deteriorated English ones. The miserable specimens of bulls I see in some of the jails in India will ruin the cows covered by them. If these jail dairies had first-class Hissar cows and bulls they could help a great deal in distributing good young bulls over the country, and thus greatly improve the country cattle. If the jail authorities would follow the methods I have suggested they would soon improve their dairies and would find a ready sale for all the bull-calves they could produce. The natives will willingly pay from Rs. 20 to Rs. 40 for a good eight to ten months old bull-calf of the Hissar breed, and Rs. 100 or more for one between one and two years old.

CHAPTER XI.

BULLOCKS.

Bullocks and Buffaloes are the only animals used in the plough in India. They are also very largely used in the cart and carriage. Very often, keeping one's own bullocks and cart is a great saving and convenience.

The points in a good bullock are the same as those in a good bull, only, bullocks are not so heavy as bulls, and are much more active and fiery, and walk faster. When their tails or hips are touched they run.

The creamy white are considered to be generally not very strong, but I have had a creamy white bull that was perfect in every respect. Very large dewlaps and very much loose skin under the stomach of bullocks are considered signs of weakness.

When a bull is castrated his form undergoes somewhat of a change, and he sometimes looks like a cow.

Food. – Working bullocks should have the same quality of food as bulls, but half as much in quantity. Instead of two meals, three should be given: one at daybreak, the second at 1 p.m., and the last at sunset, when they are tied up for the night. They should never be fed immediately before or after hard work. An interval of two hours should be allowed between the meals and work.

Grooming and Cleaning.—Bullocks need to be properly groomed every day and kept perfectly clean, and their utensils and house should be kept as clean as those of cows. Bullocks should not be exposed to the midday sun and heavy rains and cold sharp winds.

Water.—Bullocks and bulls should have plenty of clean drinking-water.

Rearing Bullocks.—When a calf is reared for the plough and, especially, the cart, he should be allowed the whole or the greater portion of his mother's milk, and, in addition, a liberal supply of good wholesome prepared food. The beautiful animals we sometimes see in carriages up-country were never deprived of any portion of their mothers' milk, and were well cared for and fed from the beginning.

CHAPTER XII.

DRY COWS.

Selling Dry Cows.—Some persons think dry cows a great trouble and expense to keep, and as soon as their cows run dry they sell them. Unless a cow is an inferior one, or has been spoiled, is diseased, or has become barren, she should not be sold because she has run dry. As has been said, a good cow will amply repay her owner.

Keeping dry cows that are in calf is not a great expense. Dry ones sell for from a quarter to half the price of cows in milk. The cost of keeping a dry cow until she calves will not exceed the difference in price between a dry one and one in full milk, and the owner will be fully repaid by the improved quality and quantity of the milk, due to proper care and management.

A good cow giving from ten to twelve *seers* of milk will cost, in Calcutta, about Rs. 150. She will milk for 300 days, and average 14 lbs. of milk a day. The yield for 300 days will be 4200 lbs. The value of this at 12 lbs. per rupee is Rs. 350. The cost of food and keep for the period will be Rs. 200. Now if the cow is properly managed she will yield the following profit. If sold when dry—

Dr.

Purchase of cow	Rs. 150
Cost of food, etc.	200
Total	350

Cr.

Value of milk	Rs. 350
Value of calf at ten months . .	20
Sale of cow to butcher	50
Total	420
Expenditure	350
Profit	70

If kept till next calving—

Dr.

Purchase of cow	Rs. 150
Cost of food, etc., for ten months .	200
Extra cost for four months when dry .	12
Total	362

Cr.

Value of milk	Rs. 350
Value of calf	20
Value of cow when she calves again .	150
Total	520
Expenditure	362
Profit	158

So we see that to keep a cow for the second year will yield more than double the profit that she yields if kept only one year. Of course this presupposes proper management. It will never pay a dairyman in India to fatten cows for the butcher. Every cow he has to sell is so much loss, and every cow he is able to keep and breed from is so much gain.

Advantage.—" It is advantageous to buy a cow before she calves, as you then get the whole of her milk; you have also the management of her before and after calving, and if she be in skilful hands she will give more milk than she would do if mismanaged.

" It is also well to get her accustomed to her attendants and her stall before she calves, as any change of quarters afterwards will make her fret, and this will at once tell on her milk. If the calf is not very young, any check of this kind will lessen her milk permanently. So it often happens that the purchaser of a cow in milk complains that the cow does not give as much milk as he was led to suppose she did, the reason being that the milk has been lessened by the fretting of the cow on changing hands. The rest and care will make the cow the better milker when she calves."—*Cows in India.*

Food.—" It is difficult to decide when to reduce a cow's feed from full feed to the spare diet of a dry cow. When a cow is in calf, and is going off her milk, and you have no other cow giving milk, or need her milk for butter, continue to feed her up; but if you have sufficient milk from other cows, or if the quantity she gives is not worth the expense of feeding her, it is better to put her on spare diet and leave her calf loose to drink what she gives. It will strengthen the calf and do the cow good."—*Cows in India.*

Dry cows must not have grain or any kind of food that fattens much. Fat in a cow is a serious defect; it makes her liable to slipping her calf, and also becoming barren.

A dry cow should have plenty of grazing during the day, and some cut grass, hay, or *bhoosa*, with half a *seer* of bran, and half a *chittack* of salt, to munch during the night; but on no account give her any mustard *khully* or other heating food. She should be rather thin to within a few weeks of her time of calving, when she will pick up of herself, if she gets a sufficient quantity of grass. If, on the other hand, the cow is starved, and allowed to get into bad condition, the calf will be weak and sickly.

Over-feeding.—"Over-feeding when a cow is not in milk makes the food run to fat, and if a cow's food once begins to do this, it will continue to do so when she is fed up after calving, and in a short time she will be fit only for the butcher; though she may have a fat udder and a large belly her milk will be scanty. But if the good food comes at calving with the fresh milk, all the food goes to milk, as the system has become accustomed to spare diet, and being healthy her muscles will improve, but she will not put on fat. If she is allowed to get fat before calving, her calf will be born puny."—*Cows in India.*

Care.—Cows in calf should have plenty of exercise; but great care should be taken that they do not fight with other cows or meet with any accident. They must not be allowed to jump or run, and they must not be driven fast or jerked. They should be groomed and washed gently, and kept clean and dry; cows during pregnancy are very delicate, and if neglected or hurt will become ill or slip the calf.

Cleanliness about their food, water, utensils, and house is just as essential as when they are milking.

Time of Pregnancy.—The time a cow is in calf is about 290 days; age and condition of health make a slight difference. The calf quickens between the fourth and fifth month.

Exercise.—Cows that are in calf must not be kept tied up all the day. They should be allowed to graze in the compound or fields near the house, or else they should be tied out in some open place with ropes at least 40 feet long. Exercise is absolutely necessary for cows that are in calf. If they do not get it they will suffer at the time of calving.

The reason why so many calves are still-born, or die soon after birth, is that the cows are allowed to become too fat. Over-feeding and want of exercise will cause a cow to grow fat. Heating food, such as oilcake and certain grains, will cause the cow to throw off and wish to go to the bull again. Sometimes a cow will, without throwing off, get into heat and take the bull; this will injure the calf and cause miscarriage.

The calf of a fat, over-fed cow will be small and weak or deformed, and not live long.

Young bulls and barren cows, and also cows that are in heat, will worry cows that are in calf and injure them.

CHAPTER XIII.

MANAGEMENT OF COWS WHEN CALVING.

LITTLE needs to be done for a cow before the time of calving, beyond attending to her food, rest, and exercise.

Signs of the Time.—When a cow is within a few days of calving, her shape will undergo a change; she will become hollow just beneath the hip bones, and her stomach will appear as if sunk down towards the chest; in the case of an old cow it is very evident that a great change has taken place in the position of the calf. Some animals evince uneasiness and irritation of the bowels and bladder by the constant motion of the tail, and by the ineffectual attempts made to dung; the vagina becomes loosened and increased in size, and a white or pale straw-coloured glairy discharge exudes from it some two or three weeks before the time. As soon as this change is observed the cow must not be sent out to graze, but must be kept at home in order that the event may not be unduly hurried from any unforeseen cause. If a cow calves away from home she runs the risk of catching a chill. Some cows calve very quickly, even the very day the change is observed, while others may not do so for a week or more. Keeping them quiet has a very beneficial effect upon them. About ten or fifteen days before calving the udder increases, and sometimes becomes full of milk, and the milk-vein is distended. A cow in this state is very liable to take a chill; she should be kept dry and away from draughts, and should not be bathed.

If the udder is very much enlarged and the milk-vein distended, it should be emptied every morning and evening. Unless this is done inflammation of the udder may set in, and the cow get milk-fever, and both cow and calf suffer much. I once lost a very fine cow and calf from neglecting to do this. If the cow is once milked she must be milked regularly every day, and every drop extracted. After milking, rub some mustard oil on the udder.

Labour Approaching.—"An hour or two before the event, the face of the cow will bear an anxious look; the eyes will be bright and staring and hollow, indicative of pain. As soon as the cow shows these signs, she should be taken into her house and kept quiet; some straw should be spread on the floor, and she should be given a good supply of soft green grass to amuse herself and keep her from fretting. Her keeper should remain close at hand, but be careful not to disturb her unnecessarily, nor sit and watch her from where she can see him. She will eat a little at times when out of pain. When she begins to sit down and get up, as if uneasy, the man should stay with her until the calf is born, and afterwards he should prevent her from getting up until the calf is quite clear of its mother."—*Cows in India.*

Progress of Labour.—"The actual progress of labour becomes evident by the protrusion of the membranes, or bag of water as it is termed, which breaks; the animal lies down, and, after a while, turns flat on her side, generally the left. The fore feet of the calf may now be seen protruding through the vulva; and, as labour advances, the head comes forth closely applied over the fore feet, with the chin resting on the knees, and the back of the calf parallel to that of the cow. After the head makes its appearance there is a short respite of some two or three minutes, and the trunk and hind extremities, stretched at full length, are pushed out by the expulsive efforts of the uterus, assisted by the diaphragm and abdominal muscles. A few seconds after the birth of the calf the cow sits up, and then, rising on her legs, commences to lick her calf, which she does incessantly for some time, the calf the while lying still, stretched out and gasping. Gradually it raises its head, draws its fore feet under it, and begins to make ineffectual efforts to get on its legs, which it eventually succeeds in doing. It then totters about, by degrees attains firmness on its legs, and after a short time is able to support its body steadily."—*A Manual of Indian Cattle and Sheep.*

Assistance Needed.—In most cases no assistance whatever is needed, nature accomplishing her course with perfect safety to mother and young. Occasionally a cross-birth may occur, and surgical assistance be necessary. In such cases a doctor should be called in at once.

At the moment of calving most of the natives know what to do, and are good nurses if the birth be a natural one. Where they fail is in the management before and after birth.

Treatment of the Cow after the Birth of the Calf.—When the cow and calf have been attended to, a quarter of a *seer* of *goor*, a quarter of a *seer* of dried ginger, and one *chittack* of *huldi* should be obtained. The ginger and *huldi* should be well ground, and mixed with the *goor* and some flour, and the cow should be given half the mixture at once, as it helps to clear away the after-birth, and reduce the after-pains, which trouble and weaken some well-bred cows very much; many of the best milkers are very delicate, and suffer much at the time of calving. The remainder of the mixture of ginger and *goor* should be given about six hours afterwards; no more should be given, as it will be hurtful as soon as the milk flows. (See Book II., Chapter III.)

Great care is needed to prevent the cow's vagina and the calf's navel from becoming sore and getting blown by flies. They must be washed with warm water, and, after drying them thoroughly with a clean soft cloth, the following ointment must be applied:—Sweet oil or mustard oil, 4 *chittacks*; camphor, 1 *tola*; spirits of turpentine, 1 *chittack*. This must be done every morning and evening for a week or ten days.

Drink and Food.—"Care must be taken that the cow has nothing to drink, and that she has a warm coat thrown over her, or she is very apt to catch cold during the first hours succeeding the birth of the calf. If she is doing well the less you disturb her the better; but if her eyes become glassy and of a steel colour when the light is thrown on them, and the hollows above them deepen, she is in pain, and about four hours after the birth she should have a hot bran mash, rather sloppy, which will fill and warm her inside, and quell the pain. This should be continued for the first three days, as it assists the milk to come, keeps her inside warm, and opens her bowels. For the first day she should have no water, and then warm water for a week; this is a point to be very careful about, as a draught of cold water will chill her milk, and may produce swollen udder and inflamed nipples — most troublesome complaints, resulting in the cow drying up—and she suffers so much pain that she will not allow herself to be milked, nor her calf to suck."—*Cows in India.* (See Book II., Chapter III.)

For the first week the cow must not have any other food than plenty of soft green grass and one *seer* of wheat bran with a *chittack* of salt, and one *chittack* of pounded *huldi* (turmeric) added to it. This must be given twice or three times a day. For the first three days no straw should be given, and for the first week no rich food, as it may cause inflammation of the udder.

It must be remembered that cows that are large milkers are unnatural cows; they are like cultivated plants, very delicate. A common cow that gives only enough milk for her calf, may stand neglect, but a good milker will go wrong in no time.

Illness.—Anything wrong with a cow at such a time must be promptly attended to. (See Book II., Chapter III.)

Falling of the Womb.—See Book II., Chapter III.

Milking.—About an hour or so after a cow has calved she should be milked, and the calf set to suck. The calf should be loose with the mother, and allowed to suck her at pleasure; the sucking will open the milk-vessels, and bring the milking-machinery into play; the calf being hungry, will suck hard, and draw off pain from the cow But the cow must be milked regularly three times a day for three days after calving, and every drop of milk extracted each time. An hour before she is milked the calf should be separated from the mother. On the third day the real flow of milk sets in, the udder increases, and the milk is quite fit to use for puddings and butter; the butter will be large in quantity, and rich in colour and flavour. The milk should not be given to babies until the calf is three weeks old. After the seventh day, and until the end of the first month after calving, the milk will not produce much butter. When the calf is allowed to be with the mother, great care is needed lest the cow crush the calf. I allow the calf to suck for half an hour or an hour, and then shut it up in its own room for an hour or two, when I let it out again for another half an hour or so, and again put it away. I do this throughout the day and night for the first fortnight.

CHAPTER XIV.

CALVES, THEIR VALUE, MANAGEMENT, AND HOUSE.

Value of Calves.—The value of a calf depends much upon its breed, just as a thoroughbred colt is of greater value than a common one. The price of a year-old calf varies from Rs. 3 to Rs. 50, and of a two-year-old one from Rs. 6 to Rs. 100. A heifer or bull from two and a half to three years old will fetch from Rs. 8 to Rs. 200, according to the breed and qualities of the animal. The common village cattle are of very little value.

A bull or bullock-calf will fetch more than a cow-calf will. The price of a cow is highest after she has had her first calf, and the price of a bull as well as a bullock is highest when he is between three and four years of age.

Some calves are inferior and not worth the trouble and expense of rearing; such should be sold as soon as their mothers stop milking and refuse to allow them to suck. But if a calf is a good one, it should be kept to replenish the stock. The cost of its keep and food will not exceed its value.

Food and Care.—It is no economy to starve or neglect the calf. If it gets out of condition and becomes sickly, its growth and development will be affected, and its value materially lessened. Whereas if it dies, the mother's supply of milk is sure to decrease and the cow liable to be utterly spoiled. A calf should never be deprived of its mother's milk. For the first month after its birth the calf will not eat anything, and if not allowed sufficient of its mother's milk it will be seriously injured. The calf should not be separated from its mother for more than three hours at a time until it is twenty-one days old. After the twenty-first day the calf should be kept apart from the mother until she is milked, but should be allowed to suck for three hours after the cow has been milked. This should be done until the calf is two months old and can eat properly, then it need remain with the mother for an hour in the morning and an hour in the evening only.

I do not advocate the English method of treating calves. The Indian cow will not allow her calf to be taken from her. If it is done, she will never milk as well or for as long a period as she would if she were allowed her calf. English cows have generations of training at the back of them, and the separation from their calves does not injure them. It will take generations of training to make the Indian cow do without her calf. I do not advise anyone to try it. If properly treated the cow will give more milk with her calf than she will do without it.

When a calf is ten days or a fortnight old, it should be allowed some finely ground gram, wheat, or barley, and green *doob* grass every morning and evening. When three weeks old some wheat, barley, or gram, ground and soaked, mixed with some cut fresh *doob* grass, should be given to it three times a day. But on no account give the little thing dry bran and straw, as so many people do. Until the calf is two months old it should be allowed plenty of ground gram, etc., and green grass. For the first three weeks or month it will not eat much, but if given food it will nibble at it and soon learn to eat and like it.

As it grows bigger, increase the quantity of food and add a little sweet linseed oilcake to it. Mustard-seed oilcake is positively injurious to young calves. Salt and sulphur should be given to the calf from the beginning. Over-feeding is bad; ¼ of a *seer* of grain, ¼ of a *seer* of wheat bran, and ¼ of a *seer* of linseed oilcake every morning, and the same in the evening, is sufficient for a calf until it is between two and three months old, when gradually increase the quantity, but a liberal supply of tender green grass should be always allowed. Pure drinking-water should be given *ad libitum.* When a calf is between three and four months old, I reduce the quantity of grain and increase the oilcake, until at six months of age it receives only oilcake. A calf six months old should get 1½ *seer*, and when a year old 2 *seers* of oilcake a day.

The best time to feed the calves is after the cows have been milked and the calves separated from them. Regularity in feeding is indispensable.

Tying up Calves.—Little calves should never be tied up; if tied they should not be kept so long. They must be kept loose in a shed or room with an enclosure where they may run about.

House.—The calves must be kept separate from the other cattle, and their room kept clean, dry, and warm, and properly ventilated. The flooring of the calves' room must be *pucca*, and thoroughly scrubbed every morning and evening. A calf needs at least 5 feet by 4 feet of room. Dry straw should be spread on the floor for them.

Shelter from Sun and Rain.—Calves should not be exposed to the midday sun, or rain, and should be sheltered from the cold north and east winds. They are very delicate creatures, and any neglect may prove fatal.

On no account should calves be allowed to sit on wet or damp ground or grass.

Ticks and Lice.—Calves must be kept absolutely free from ticks and lice. Regular brushing will keep them free from vermin. Little calves should not be bathed.

Older Calves.—When bull-calves are six months old they should be tied up and fed. Heifers should be tied up and fed when they are four or five months old, but not kept tied all the day. Bull-calves should be very liberally fed; the quantity of their food should be continually increased, until at two years of age they receive the same quantity of food as prescribed for bulls.

Careful Treatment.—A great deal of care is needed in the management of calves. The temper and habits of cows and bullocks depend a great deal upon the treatment they have received when calves. If you want good milch-cows, then observe the following, taken from the *American Farmer*:—

"*Treat the Cows kindly.*—Here is a bit of gospel truth which should be heeded, especially by dairymen. Animals, like human beings, will respond to kindness, and on a dairy-farm this is one of the greatest essentials to success. You cannot begin too early in training your calves to come at your call, and to submit to handling and petting. Accustom them to familiarity with persons, but never permit them to be vexed or irritated, if you do not want them to become ill-natured cows. While good blood is of the greatest importance, still if not properly trained the highest satisfaction will not be attained. A good animal may be spoiled by bad management. Good feed, good care, and petting will naturally aid in securing good results."

This is very true about heifers. I have seen cows that would not allow themselves to be tied or touched, and were as wild as jungly cattle. Though of good breeds, they were fit only for the butcher. Their bad tricks were attributable to nothing else but bad management when calves.

Male calves that are intended for the plough or cart should not be treated like the heifers. The less they are tied up and petted and handled the better; their backs or tails should not be touched. Handling and petting bull-calves makes them very tame and slow in harness, and considerably lessens their value.

Heifers need special attention; very often they are neglected and receive neither proper food nor shelter, consequently they are small and deformed, and are unfit for milking purposes. Then again, some heifers are so highly fed that they become barren. I have known cases in which all the efforts of the owners have failed to make the animals productive. These heifers come into season and take the bull, but never get into calf. They have been spoiled by overheating and too much food. Heifers should be kept in good condition, but never allowed to grow very fat. They should be fed on the same kind of food as milk-cows, but should not be allowed so much oilcake or grain, and on no account any cotton-seed. Good green grass and hay should be given in abundance. The food should be prepared in the same way as food for milch-cows. Some salt and an unlimited supply of pure drinking-water are essential to the animal's health.

Why so many Calves die.—A large number of calves die from sheer neglect and mismanagement. They are deprived of their mothers' milk, and insufficient and unwholesome food is given to them; they are exposed to sudden changes of weather, and not sheltered from the cold and damp at night, or heat in the day; they are allowed to become covered with lice and ticks, and their houses are kept unclean.

If the calves are cared for and properly reared it will help the cow to give more milk and milk for a longer time, and the calf will repay all that is spent on its care and food.

CHAPTER XV.

POINTS IN A GOOD CALF.

"*A good bull-calf* should have loose skin running from his chin down his dewlap and round his chest and along his belly; his eyes should be far apart, and his forehead broad; his nose short and turned up; his joints large and looking swollen. The size of the joints is an indication of his eventual growth, and the better bred he is the more ungainly will his joints be. The shorter his neck the greater will be his strength. His hair should be soft, long, and rather curly. If he is in good health his nose will be wet and shining. An ill-bred calf will have a narrow head, very long ears, small eyes rather close together, long neck, small joints, and legs tapering away at the feet like a goat's."—*Cows in India.*

"*A good cow-calf* should have much the same points as a bull-calf, but her head will not be so broad or her neck so short; and instead of the long dewlap, she should have, if of a good milking breed, lots of yellow wrinkled skin between her legs where the udder will be in time to come, and she will have well-developed teats, even when only a few hours old; and the best milkers will always have silky hair."—*Cows in India.*

CHAPTER XVI.

CASTRATING CALVES.

Castrating when Young.—In Europe, calves as a rule are castrated between the first and third month after birth. The advantage of the operation at this early age consists in the improvement of the animal in form, size, and the propensity to fatten, while it also renders him docile and generally useful as a working bullock. The natives of India, on the contrary, wait till the animal is from two to five years old, that is, between the time when it has from two to six permanent teeth.

Mode of Castration.—Natives generally castrate without cutting the animal at all. The bull is thrown down and its four legs are tied together; then the scrotum is drawn out and freely handled for a few minutes to relax it; after which stout wooden rollers about 15 inches in length, and 1½ inch in diameter, are tied tightly at one end, and passed between the scrotum containing the gland and the body of the animal. One gland is next pushed up towards the abdomen, and the other retained in the scrotal sack; the rollers are then drawn down and the free ends are tied together. A man sits in front and presses the gland tightly against the rollers till it bursts within its sack or the bag of the scrotum, when he seizes the broken gland between the fingers of both his hands, and kneads it well till it becomes broken up into a soft pulp. The other gland is next drawn out between the rollers and crushed in like manner, and a little cow-dung or *huldi* (turmeric) is lastly smeared over the scrotum. At the same time, the cartilage between the nostrils is perforated with a sharp wooden or steel needle, and a cord a quarter of an inch thick is put through as a nose-string. This string is put through the nose and over the head at the back of the horns, another string is put round the neck as a collar, then an iron or brass ring is put round the nose-string and the collar, and a string is attached to the ring as a bridle. No further treatment is ever necessary. The animal is well in ten days. I certainly think well of this mode of operation, and have had a number of my young bulls castrated in this way, but many people prefer cutting.

Effect of this Process.—There is no wound or subsequent discharge and inflammation, as is the case after cutting. The scrotum swells, and in ten days or a fortnight the whole gland becomes absorbed and only the empty sack remains. This process of castrating is never attended with any danger, nor is it so painful as the cutting process. The animals further retain their masculine form to a certain extent. When a calf is cut, it soon loses its masculine form, and as it grows larger, it looks somewhat like a cow; but when the glands are crushed the change in form is not so great, though the animal may not become as large as it would have if it had been cut.

Proper Time to Castrate.—A calf should be cut when it is between two and six months old, but a calf should not be crushed before it is between eighteen months and two years old.

Great Care in the Operation.—When the glands are crushed great care must be taken that they are very thoroughly crushed up, otherwise the animal will occasionally prove troublesome among the cows. When the calf is cut, care must be taken that the sore is not fly-blown or allowed to fester.

The evil of late castration consists in the young bulls being allowed to roam at large with the cows. The native breeders never think of separating the bulls from the cows. Even if there be a good bull in the herd, he is over-reached by those young bulls, from their lightness of carcase and activity in serving the cows.

CHAPTER XVII.

TAKING THE BULL.

A very important Matter.—This is a critical moment with owners of cows, because it is a matter of very great importance, and any mistake at this time will very seriously affect the profit to be derived from the cow.

Before putting a cow to the bull, the owner must be certain that she is not already in calf. If a cow in calf be put to the bull, it will very seriously injure her and will be certain to cause a miscarriage of the young one. Many people think that a cow in calf will not show any signs of being in heat, and the bull will not cover her. This is a mistake. I have known cows that have progressed as far as six or seven months in pregnancy to worry other cows by riding them; and I have known bulls to follow and worry cows that have far advanced in pregnancy. But such a mistake as putting a cow in calf to the bull can be very effectually prevented.

Early Months of Pregnancy.—In the early months

of pregnancy it is difficult to decide if a cow is or is not in calf. It is most necessary to know for certain, both to her lying fallow when she ought to be in calf, and also to prevent her being put to the bull when she is already in calf, and causing much mischief.

Signs of Pregnancy.—The most certain sign of a cow carrying is a discharge from the vagina, however small. In the absence of this, it is probable that she is not in calf. In the later months, a cow's condition is quite evident from her size.

Between the fourth and fifth months of pregnancy, it can be ascertained with certainty that a cow is in calf. The calf may be felt by putting the points of the fingers hard against the right flank of the cow, when a hard lump will bound against the abdomen and be felt by the fingers; or when a bucket of cold water is drunk by the cow the calf kicks, and a convulsive motion may be observed in the flank by looking at it from behind; if the open hand is then laid upon the space between the flank and the udder, this motion may be distinctly felt.

When a Cow comes into Season.—A cow must not be put to the bull until three months after the birth of her last calf, as the womb during that period is in a relaxed state and incapable of retaining the seed, consequently she seldom conceives if she should take the bull before this period has expired. Disregarding the call of the cow at this time will do her no harm. If she calls give her some butter-milk (not sour) first thing in the morning for a few days, and a cold bath during the day. This will cool her down. But after the third month from the birth of her calf, it is very injurious to the cow to neglect the wants of nature. If she calls for the bull and is neglected, she may become barren, or slip her calf next time, which is a sign of weakness.

Rich food and over-feeding have the effect of bringing the cow into season before the proper time for it.

Some heifers take the bull when they are eighteen months old. Others again do not come into season until they are three years old. A heifer if properly fed and cared for should take the bull when she is two years and three months old.

Some cows come into season in three months from the time they have last calved. These have a calf every twelve or thirteen months. Others again milk for six or eight months before they take the bull; I had a large Hansi that milked for twelve months before she took the bull.

The Symptoms of coming into season are, abatement of milk and restlessness. The cow will be frequently dunging, staling, and bellowing. Her tail will be in constant motion, and she will have no appetite. The vagina will appear red and inflamed, and a transparent discharge will sometimes flow from it. If in the field, the cow will be riding other cows; if tied, she will stamp with her feet and pull at her rope. Some become very savage, and will butt. Others again show their state but little, often doing no more than lowing gently; these latter are apt to be neglected, as their state is not soon observed.

The time a Cow remains in Season.—These symptoms last only a few hours, sometimes only an hour, and the cow should be put to the bull immediately. Time is an object. If the cow has taken the bull and not become pregnant, the above-mentioned symptoms will return in three weeks, and continue to do so until she does conceive. A fat, over-fed cow will want to go out to the bull time after time before she is in calf. Such a cow must be somewhat reduced in condition before she will become pregnant.

Troublesome Cows.—If a cow remains more than a year without getting into calf, she should be sent out altogether to remain with the other cattle in the field, grazing and feeding with them. The company and change of air and food may have the desired effect. If a cow is troublesome about getting into calf, give her a small quantity of the refuse liquor from a native distillery; it is the juice of the *Mahowa* (none other should be given), and will often answer the purpose. This stuff should never be given to a cow in milk, as it is of a very heating nature and will dry up the milk. Nor should it be given to a cow in calf.

Barren cows are very troublesome. It is best to keep them separate, as they often worry other cows and spoil them. March and April are the months when nearly all cows call for the bull. So a barren cow should be carefully watched during these months, for if she calves once she may turn over a new leaf and take to calving again regularly. If a cow does not get into calf a year from the time she stops milking, or two years from the time she last calved, it is no use keeping her any longer; the probabilities are that she will never calve again.

Very often when a cow loses her calf the gowallahs resort to the practice of *phooka* to extract her milk; apart from its being a cruel and inhuman practice, a cow that has once been subjected to it will never again have a calf, her generative organs having been destroyed or injured.

Great care should be taken to select a good bull to serve the cow. A good bull of a good milking breed will generally have good milking daughters. This is a subject to which special attention should be paid. If the cow is served by a good bull, it will not only insure the production of a well-bred calf, but will also increase the quantity of the cow's milk and improve the cow.

I do not advocate English bulls for Indian cows.

The pure-bred Hissar, Nellore, or Guzerat bull will prove the best. A cross-bred bull between a short-horn cow and a Hissar, Nellore, or Guzerat bull will prove very satisfactory; but a cross between the English bull and Indian cow will not do well.

It is a great mistake to send cows out to inferior bulls. The cowman, if not watched, will put the cow to the first bull which is at hand, which may not be at all a good animal. If a good and large cow be served by a small and inferior bull, generally the serving proves unproductive. On the other hand, if a cow has been troublesome about getting into calf, if she be sent to a large and good bull she generally conceives.

As a rule cow-calves take after their fathers, and bull-calves after their mothers.

Putting the Cow to the Bull.—The most natural way is to allow the bull and cow to please themselves, and so leave them alone in an enclosure; but when cows are restless, I have found it best to tie them up to a tree between two posts and secure them so as to prevent them from jumping about, so that the bull may easily serve them and not be tired out in attempting to do so. When a cow or heifer has been served, she should be bathed in cold water, dried and tied up and left undisturbed; she will generally sit down quietly and not move for hours. It is best not to give her anything but some green grass or straw and water that day. A little soaked *Kutheela* gum should be given her.

Heifers are sometimes troublesome on account of their timidity, and may not get into calf till long after they are old enough, and have to be put to the bull many times before he succeeds in covering them. They should be tied up so as to enable the bull to serve properly.

The Sex of the Calf determined.—It has been observed that queen-bees lay female eggs first, and male eggs afterwards. So with hens, the first laid eggs give female and the last male products. Mares shown the stallion late in their periods, drop colts rather than fillies.

M. Thurz, professor in the Academy of Geneva, from the consideration of these facts, formed this law for stock-raisers: "If you wish to produce females, give the male at the first signs of heat."

A noted Swiss stock-grower, son of the President of the Swiss Agricultural Society, Canton de Vaud, under date of February 1867, certifies:—"In the first place on twenty-two successive occasions I desired to have heifers. My cows were of Schurtz breed, and my bull a pure Durham. I succeeded in these cases. Having bought a pure Durham cow, it was very important for me to have a new bull to supersede the one I had bought at great expense, without leaving to chance the production of a male. So I followed accordingly the prescription of Professor Thurz, and the success has proved once more the truth of the law. I have obtained from my Durham bull six more bulls (Schurtz-Durham) for field work; and having chosen cows of the same colour and height, I obtained perfect matches of oxen. My herd amounted to forty cows of every age.

"In short, I have made in all twenty-nine experiments after the new method, and in every one I succeeded in the production of what I was looking for, male or female. I had not one single failure; all the experiments have been made by myself, without any other person's intervention; consequently I do declare that I consider as real and certainly perfect the method of Professor Thurz."

The above plan had also been tried on farms of the French Emperor with, it is asserted, the most unvarying success.

The same plan may be adopted with animals of all descriptions.

CHAPTER XVIII.

BARREN COWS.

BECAUSE a cow has taken the bull and not become pregnant it is no proof that she is barren. Some cows, and especially the large well-bred ones, take the bull several times before they get into calf. I had a Hansi that was served five times without any satisfactory results, but the sixth time she became pregnant. Sometimes cows give much trouble and annoyance and cause much loss of time, but perseverance wins the day.

If a cow has not got into calf within two years from the time she had her last calf, she is barren, and in all probability will never calve again. It is no use whatever keeping a barren cow; she will fatten easily, and it is best to fatten her up and sell her for what she will fetch.

Causes of Sterility.—Over-feeding, or feeding on very heating food, will cause barrenness. Forcing supplies of milk by unnatural means is sure to make a cow barren. Displacement of the womb, caused by bad delivery or slinking, will cause sterility. Some organic or constitutional disease will prevent conception.

It is said, if a barren cow is allowed to remain in the herd, others in that herd will soon become barren. The disorder is infectious.

Remedy.—When a cow gives trouble about getting into calf she should be reduced in condition; she should have only green grass, hay, or dry straw to eat. This treatment alone may cure her; she should be kept loose and made to take lots of exercise. If she still continues to give trouble, give her five to ten grains of borax every day, for five or six days. If this does no good, give her five grains of ergot of rye or sabina every day for two days before and after she takes the bull. If she is not incurable this will cure her. After the cow has been served she should be kept away at a distance from the bull.

CHAPTER XIX.

AGE OF CATTLE AND NAMES AT DIFFERENT AGES.

Age.—The age of cattle is generally calculated by the growth of the permanent teeth, and also by the rings that form round the horns; but it is only after the third year that the circle on the horns becomes defined; so in calculating age by the rings, allowance should be made for three years; when an animal has six rings it is eight years old (see plates). Of the two systems, that of judging by the teeth is by far the more reliable; even with this system, it is difficult to tell the age of a calf before it sheds two of its central milk teeth; and again there is a difficulty when the animal completes teething at the fifth year. At six years of age the eight permanent teeth are complete and attain a uniform level, and the mouth is said to be complete, literally what the natives call *poora* in Hindi, and *pooro* or *poorno* in Bengali, when the animal has attained its prime. After this, the animal is supposed to decline or approach the age when its value decreases. After the sixth year all is guesswork, and nothing can be affirmed decidedly. Those,

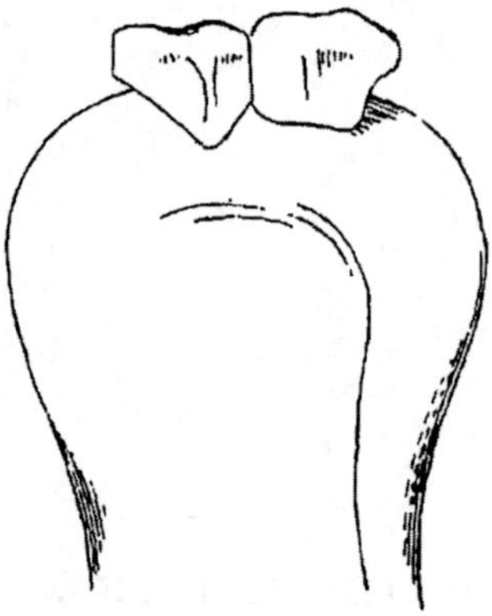

BIRTH.

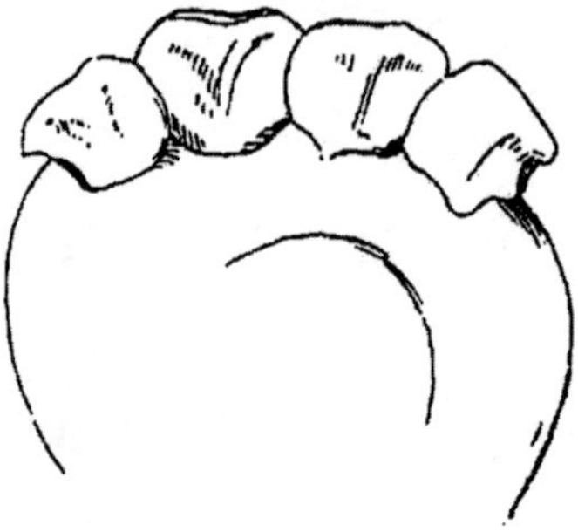

SECOND WEEK.

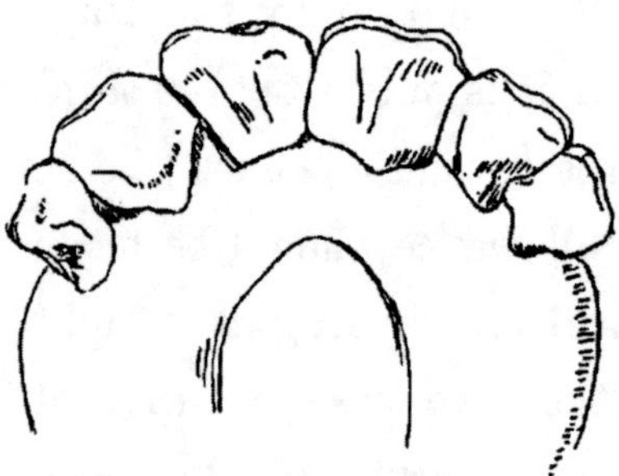

THIRD WEEK.

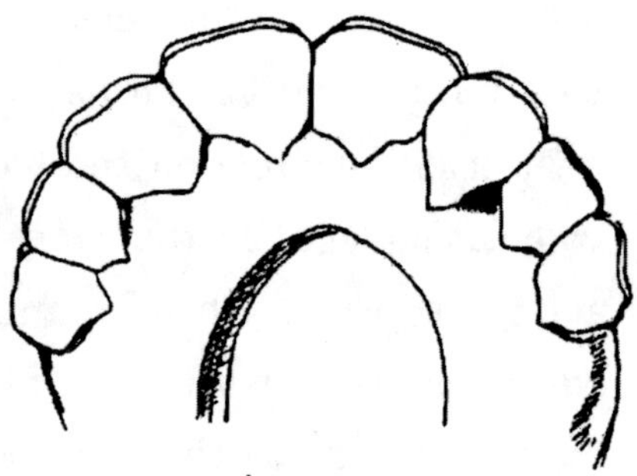

FOURTH WEEK.

EIGHT MONTHS.

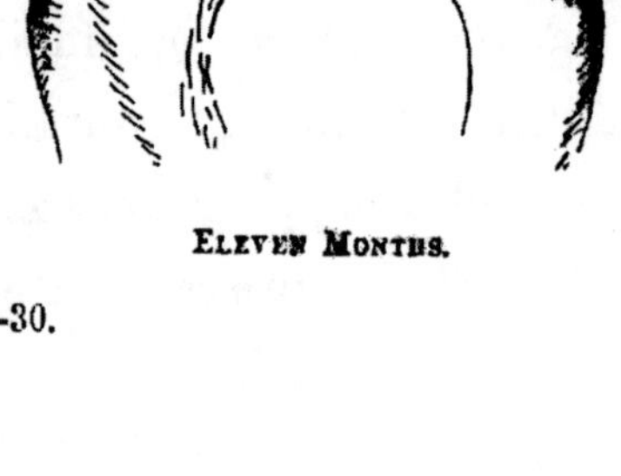

ELEVEN MONTHS.

FIGS. 25–30.

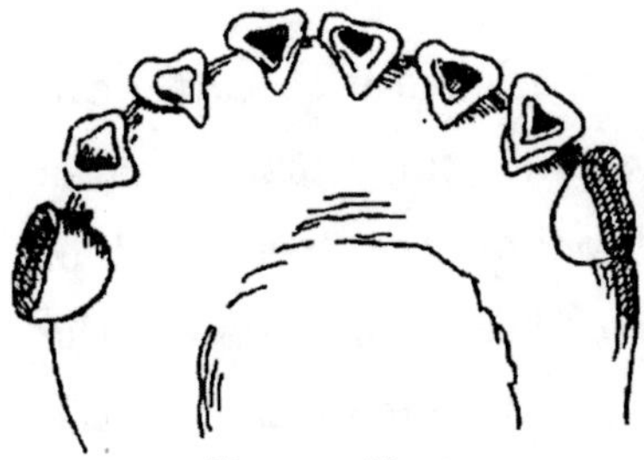

FIFTEEN MONTHS.

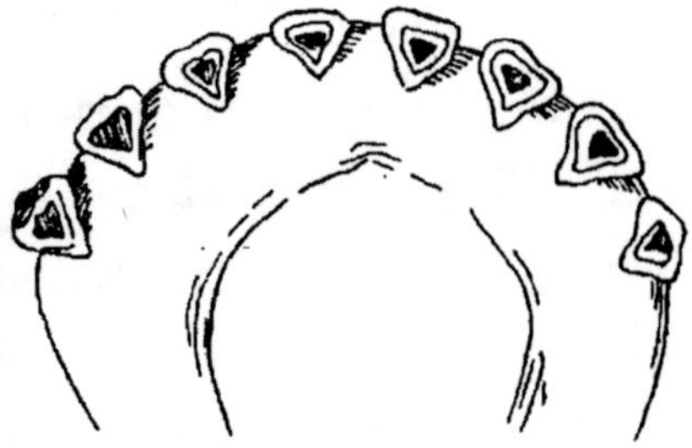

EIGHTEEN MONTHS.

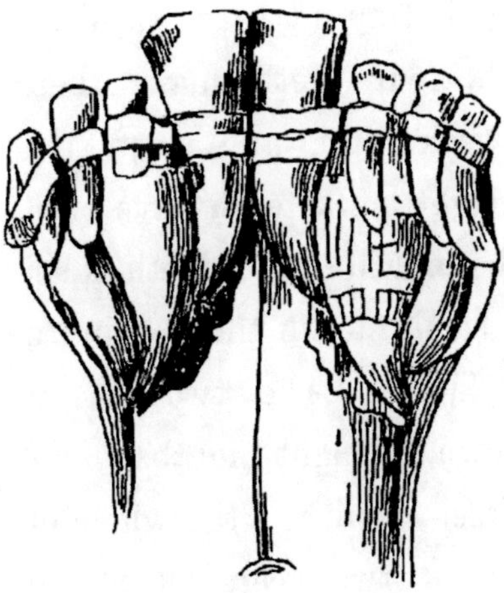

TWO YEARS.

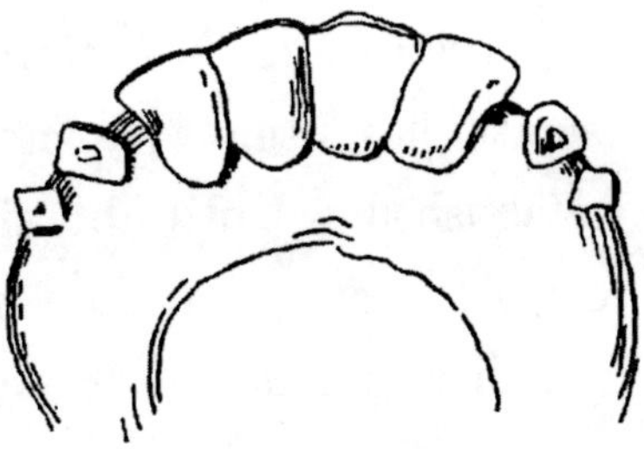

THIRD YEAR.

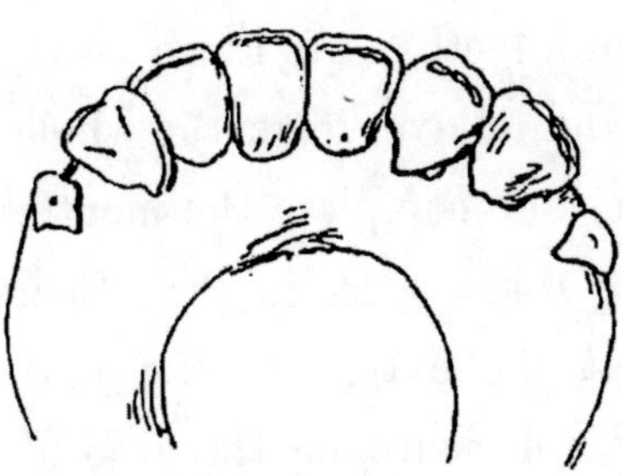

FOURTH YEAR.

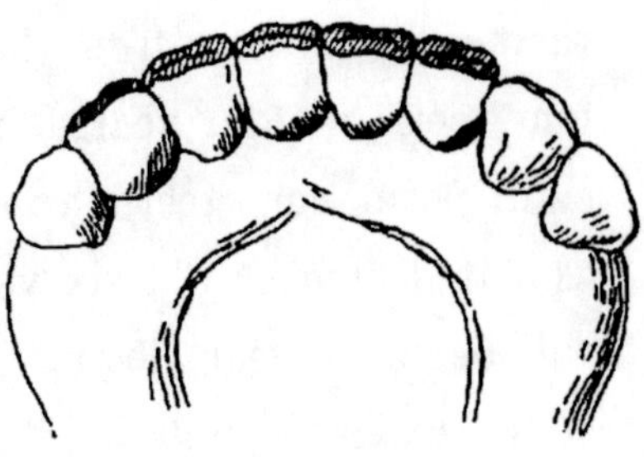

FIFTH YEAR.

FIGS. 31–36.

however, who have extensive experience with cattle can tell the age even after the sixth year with tolerable correctness. Careful examination of the teeth and of the extent to which they have been worn down, the marks on the horns, and the general appearance of the animal itself, frequently help to determine the question.

At birth there are two central milk teeth, or incisors in the lower jaw, the upper continuing bare. During the second week after birth, four teeth make their appearance; in the third week, six; and when the mouth has been completed, eight milk teeth have been established. Until the sixth month these teeth keep clean and even, but after the sixth month they begin to get discoloured and to wear down. The two central incisors first begin to wear down at eight months; four at twelve months; six at fifteen months; the whole of the eight teeth are well worn at two years, when also two of the central incisors are shed and replaced by permanent teeth, which are readily distinguished by their size and form from the milk teeth. At three years, four teeth, at four years, six, and at five years, the whole eight permanent teeth appear, and complete the mouth, as stated above. At six years of age these in their turn will begin to wear down. But the extent of the wear of the teeth depends in a great measure on the kind of food the animal has been having. Cattle—bulls, bullocks, and cows—attain to a good age when taken care of, and the reproducing powers of bulls and cows are retained for a long period.

The cow breeds when she is two years old, and continues to do so until she is twenty years of age; the bull is used for breeding purposes when he is three years old, and

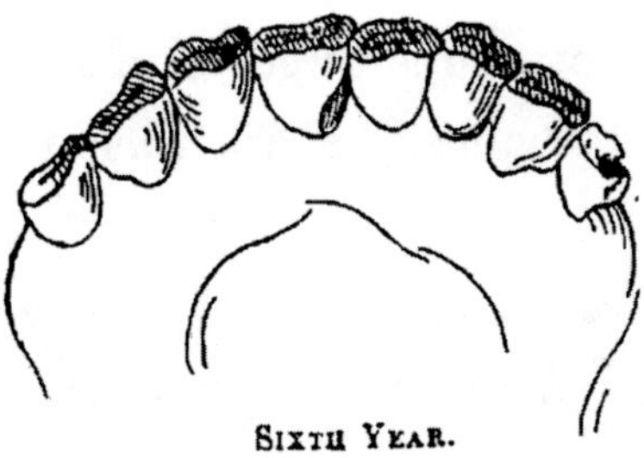

SIXTH YEAR.

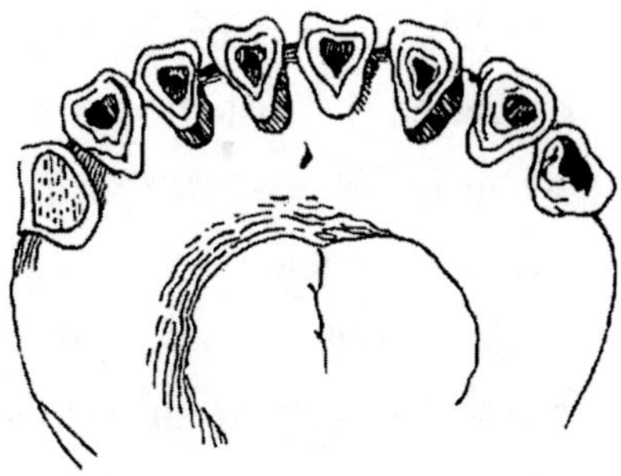

TENTH YEAR.

AGE SHOWN BY RINGS FOUND ON THE HORN.

FIGS. 37–39.

renders his best services until he is eight years old. After that he should not be used for breeding from, but ought to be put to the plough or cart. Sometimes he is used before he is three years old, but this is ruinous; if he be left until he is three years of age it will repay in the offspring.

Names of Cattle at different Ages.—The names given to cattle are as follows:—A new-born animal is termed "a calf," the male "a bull-calf," and the female "a quey," "cow-calf," or "heifer"; a gelded animal is called a "stot-calf." When a calf is a year old it is called "a yearling." When a heifer bears a calf she is called "a cow," which name she retains ever after. A bull when castrated is called "a steer" until he is three years old, when he is styled "an ox" or "bullock," which name is never changed.

A heifer or cow that has received the bull is said to have been served or covered. A cow that has not conceived or that has miscarried her young is an "eill," and one that has ceased milking is called a "yeld - cow." When in milk a cow is termed a "milk" or "milch-cow."

Native Names.—A calf is called a "butchroo" in Hindi, and a "bachoor" in Bengali. A bull-calf is a "shār-butchroo" in Hindi, and "shār-bachoor" in Bengali. A cow-calf is a "buckun" in Hindi, and a "bokkon" in Bengali. A stot-calf is a "buddhia butchroo" in Hindi, and a "bollod bachoor" in Bengali, and a steer a "bial" in Hindi, and a "bollod or damra" in Bengali. A cow is a "gai," and a bull a "shār" (nasal sh) in both Hindi and Bengali.

CHAPTER XX.

PRICE OF CATTLE.

THE prices of cattle vary a great deal in different parts of the country, and at different seasons of the year. Cattle in their own districts are cheap, but the farther they are removed from home the greater their price.

In Bengal the ryots sell off their cattle after they have finished their ploughing in the hot weather. From May to the end of September the fields are all under cultivation, and there is no fodder for the cattle, consequently during these months they die off in large numbers from starvation and disease. Most of the ryots sell their cattle at this season, and buy again in October and November. The prices go up in October and continue good till the end of February. Many ryots, again, sell their cattle during the rains to enable them to pay their land rents. From October to December they reap their crops and are flush with cash, so they can again buy cattle.

Prices of Cows.—The prices of cows vary according to their breed and the quantity and quality of the milk they give. In Calcutta the standard price of a good cow in full milk, with a calf under a month old, is as follows. If a large well-bred animal, at the rate of Rs. 12 to Rs. 13 per *seer* for every *seer* of milk she gives in twenty-four hours. If a medium-sized well-bred cow, Rs. 10 to Rs. 11 per *seer* for every *seer* of milk she gives in twenty-four hours; and if a small cow, at the rate of from Rs. 8 to Rs. 10 per *seer*. Thus a large cow giving ten *seers* of milk a day will fetch Rs. 120, and a small one giving five *seers* a day Rs. 40. I have known some large cows to sell at the rate of Rs. 16 per *seer* for the milk they yielded in twenty-four hours. Sometimes when people are leaving the place and cannot take their cattle with them, they will sell them for far below the standard price. Cows can also be got cheap at auction sales, but the buyer has to take his chance.

In the Mofussil the prices of cows in milk are very much below the prices of the same animals in cities and towns. Cows are comparatively cheap in their own districts. The cows that sell for Rs. 120 in Calcutta, can be bought for Rs. 60 in Northern India. A cow is at its best value when it is between three and five years old, or with its second calf.

By large cows I mean cows of the Hansi, Nellore, Nagouri, or Guzerati breed; and by medium, good cross-breds: and by small, good common cows of the district.

When cows run dry their value of course decreases;

they can be bought for from one-fourth to two-thirds the price of cows in full milk.

Prices of Bulls.—The prices of good bulls are very high; one has to pay almost a fancy price for a fine well-bred bull. A good large thoroughbred animal when three years old will sell for from Rs. 150 to Rs. 300. I have had to pay Rs. 100 for a year-old Hansi bull that was not the very best type of his breed. He was the only bull to be had at the place.

Prices of Bullocks.—The prices of good bullocks are also high. Good Bengali bullocks will fetch as much as Rs. 40 or Rs. 60 per pair. The common ones sell for from Rs. 14 to Rs. 30 per pair. Good cross-breds will bring as much as Rs. 80 to Rs. 120 per pair. First-class thoroughbreds will sell for as high as Rs. 200 to Rs. 400 per pair.

Breed, age, size, and strength make a great difference in the value of the animal. A bullock is at his best value when he is between three and six years old.

Prices of Calves, see Chapter XIV.

CHAPTER XXI.

MILK.

The quantity of milk obtainable varies considerably according to the breed of the cow, the kind of food she has, and the time after calving. A thoroughbred well-cared-for cow will give much more milk than a common one, or a badly-cared-for high caste one. Some cows have given as much as eighteen *pucca seers* of milk a day, but if a cow gives from ten to twelve *seers*, she is a very good one. The season and frequency with which a cow is milked also affects the quantity. When a cow is milked twice a day the secretion is richer and contains more butter than when milked oftener. Climate also affects the yield of milk; cold and damp are objectionable. A rich, dry soil is very favourable.

Cows that are tied up and fed give more and nicer milk than those that are allowed to be loose all the day.

A cow gives more and richer milk after her second calf than she did with her first. When she is eight years old her milk begins to decrease in quantity, but not always in quality.

Quality of Milk.—The milk of every cow differs in body, quality, and colour. (1) There is the yellowish, creamy milk, which contains a large proportion of fatty substance necessary for butter. (2) Then there is the thick heavy white milk, which contains a great deal of casein suitable for cheese, junkets, curds, etc. (3) The thin bluish milk is sweet and nice, but does not produce much cream, butter, or curd. The last is the best for children and invalids. In good milk there should be at least four *chittacks* of curd, and one *chittack* of butter to every *seer*.

While the calf is very young the milk will be thin, but will get richer as the calf grows older. As a cow goes out of milk, the butter obtained from her milk will not lessen as rapidly as the milk itself does: the smaller quantity of milk will on account of its richness give a larger proportion of butter, and sometimes even when nearly dry a respectable quantity of butter will be yielded.

Milk from a cow when she is in season or near her time for calving is not good for children.

The milk of a cow immediately after calving is not fit for use. It is called calustrum. An hour after the cow has calved she ought to be milked and the milk thrown away; after this the calf should be allowed to suck the mother and drink all it can draw. Until the third day the calf should be allowed to draw all it can, and the milk left must be drawn out and may be used for butter, but should never be given to children. After the third day the milk may be used for tea, coffee, puddings, and butter, but is not fit for children to drink until the twenty-second day from the birth of the calf.

The Lactometer cannot be relied upon as giving any absolute standard of purity. The solids of milk are heavier than water, but the fat (butter) is lighter, and very rich milk may rank lower, as shown by the lactometer test, than milk that is really poor in quality. If you add sugar to watered milk the lactometer test will show it as pure milk. Then again, by the lactometer test the pure thin bluish milk will rank as watered milk. The gowallahs know this, and are up to the trick of making milk up to the lactometer test.

Duration of Milk.—Opinions differ as to the length of time a cow gives milk; some say, a cow should milk up to a month of her next calving, but such a cow is rarely met with. Cows are in full milk for four months on an average: from the fourth to sixth months they show signs of lessening by small degrees, during the seventh month there will be a decided decrease; they go on milking for two, three, or four, and even seven months longer, but by this time the milk will have almost dried up.

Some cows calve every year or thirteen months, and only milk for eight or nine months. Do not stop milking a cow until three or four months before the time for her to calve again. A cow if allowed to go dry early will do so again the next year, whether she calves early or not. But it is a "penny-wise pound-foolish" principle to keep on milking a cow until two months of her time to calve again.

When a cow is going off her milk, any change of food, quarters, attendants, time of milking, or the man who milks her, will often accelerate the decrease, and she will not recover herself, but the milk will stop altogether.

When a cow seems to be going off her milk, apparently without cause, it may be that she is out of sorts, and that her digestion is out of order; in such a case an ounce of the condition powder made into a ball, and given for a few days, will often restore her appetite, and give her digestion the required tone. The calf should be let loose for a day or two; its continual sucking may bring back the milk which has been checked.

Papeeta leaves and green fruit will often bring back a flow of milk if it has stopped from any disorder in the cow's health. The leaves and fruit should be pounded together, and mixed with a little flour and treacle and given in balls.

The Art of Milking.—A cow should always be fed before she is milked. No native can milk a cow without first allowing the calf to mouth the teats, as this opens the valves, and the cow seeing the calf near, allows the milk to flow; sometimes you will see both udder and milk increase rapidly in the space of a few minutes. The cow will then relieve herself as nature dictates, and, when she has done so, her calf should be tied to a peg near her head, or to her foreleg, where she can lick and fondle it while she is being milked. A kicking cow should be hobbled, but not a good-tempered one, as it is a bad habit to get them into, and may teach them to kick.

The cow should always be milked by the same man, for a change of milkers may make her restive; cows like being milked if the operator has a gentle touch. They are creatures of habit, loving peace and quiet and regular routine; if they are always fed at the same hour, and milked at the same hour, in the same place, and by the same man, they will seldom rebel.

If a cow is troublesome at milking, the milker should be changed; a good man will always have his cows quite docile, and though one may be ticklish and difficult to milk when first put under his care, in a short time he will have her quiet and patient.

Sometimes a cow's teats get chapped or inflamed, and she kicks about to let her distress be known. Chapped teats are most troublesome, and with some cows they are constitutional, but as a rule they are the result of leaving the teats wet after milking, and allowing them to dry in the open air. To avoid this, the cow's udder should be well cared for, and, from the very first, butter should be rubbed in, or a mixture of mustard-oil, wax, and fat (equal parts) boiled together into a soft ointment. It is well to rub some butter or ointment over the teats for a month after calving, as then they harden without chapping. Chapped teats are very painful and may cause the cow's milk to dry up.

If the calf nips its mother with its teeth, it must not be allowed to suck her too long at a time.

The Process of Milking.—The milking of a cow is a very simple process, but to do it successfully and correctly, without pain or annoyance to the animal, is the secret, and requires skill and experience. Milking may be performed in two ways, by stripping or nievelling. Stripping consists in seizing the teat at its base with the fore-finger and the thumb, and drawing them down to the end of the teat, pressing it lightly so as to bring away the milk it contains. Nievelling, as it is called, is effected by grasping the teat with the hand and compressing it against the palm with the fingers to drive the milk out, and then relaxing the hold to allow the teat to refill, so that by a quick succession of contraction and relaxation by the hands, the milk is soon exhausted from the udder; only large cows with large teats can be nievelled; small cows can be milked only by stripping. Every milkman prefers his own method of drawing, and it is no unusual thing to see a man use both stripping and nievelling on the same cow in the course of one single operation; habit has a great deal to do with the practice. The milking should be done quickly; the longer the milker takes in extracting the milk, the more restless the cow becomes, and the quantity of milk yielded is affected. A good milker will extract all the milk in half the time that an inexperienced man will take.

The milking utensil may be a mud, brass, or copper *lota*, tin can, or enamelled pot. Whatever the utensil may be made of, it must be kept absolutely clean.

When the calf dies there is great trouble in milking a cow. As soon as the calf dies you should try to give the cow another calf of the same age, colour, and looks as her own calf. First see that the calf is quite healthy and clean, and then take about half a *seer* of milk newly drawn from the cow, and rub it over the head, face, back, and upon the navel of the calf. The cow will smell and lick the calf, and soon allow it to suck her. Some cows will take to another calf, whereas others will not. When she will not take to another, her dead calf has to be skinned and stuffed and stuck up before her for her to look at and lick while the milking goes on. Unless this be done she will not let her milk down; but even with this device her milk will gradually lessen, as the native milker will not be able to extract every drop. As soon as the calf dies, a *mochee* or tanner should be sent for, the calf skinned, and the skin cured and stuffed and dried in the sun. If the calf has died of any contagious disease its skin will carry the contagion, so it should not be kept.

Every drop of milk must be extracted from the cow both morning and evening. After the milker has drawn away all he can, the calf must be let loose and allowed to suck, so that every drop may be extracted; any milk left in the udder tends to dry up the cow, as what is left becomes absorbed, and the flow of milk is lessened. The more you milk and the more the calf sucks, especially during the first three weeks, the more milk will be produced.

Great care must be taken not to in any way annoy or startle the cow before or during milking; any rough treatment will make her restive, and she will not allow herself to be milked. Servants need to be watched carefully, for very few natives will obey in this matter.

Forcing Supplies of Milk.—Some people give cows large drinks of hot water with bran, flour, or sugar sifted into it to make it tasty, so that they may drink largely and give a large supply of milk. Others again give large quantities of salt to the cows to produce thirst, so that they may drink water to excess. Some resort to the diabolical practice of *phooka*, in order to extract milk. The least that can be said about these unnatural means, resorted to by some unprincipled people, is, that they are highly injurious to the cow, and invariably spoil the milk. Milk produced by such methods becomes watery and is unwholesome, and causes disease in the consumer. Again, this unnatural increase is always followed by a reaction, and the supply of milk lessens considerably. Besides all this, it is most injurious to the cow. It affects her digestion, and causes much internal distress, and destroys her reproductive powers, so that she will never calve again.

FIG. 40.—MILK TUBE.

CHAPTER XXII.

CREAM.

Watered Milk.—Milk that has been watered always looks bluish, which can be detected by looking at a little in a wineglass; it appears more transparent than pure milk. But the best way of testing milk is to taste it; a little practice will enable one to detect watering. Watered milk has a wholly different flavour and feel to the tongue; it is harsh and tasteless, while pure milk is soft, sweet, and smooth. The glass bulb or lactometer for testing milk is not to be relied on: it shows the bluish pure milk, described in Chapters IV. and XXI., to be half water, whereas in reality it is pure milk. The milk of an old cow is shown to be purer than the milk of a young cow. The different kinds of food given to cows will affect the specific gravity of their milk.

Milk that has been watered will turn sour sooner than pure milk; so if milk turns sour sooner than it ought to do, you may suspect its being watered. Another way to test the milk is to let it stand for a short time: if the cream comes in a thick crust it is pure, if it breaks up on skimming and will not readily come off the milk, it has been watered, and the skimmed milk will then be of a blue colour, and look like white agate or opal. It is difficult to skim watered milk, but pure milk is easily skimmed, as the cream is thick and solid.

Cream that has been skimmed off milk that has been properly boiled and allowed to stand sufficiently long makes good butter. The natives make another kind of cream which they call *kheer* or *khoa.* It is made by simply boiling down the milk to a very thick consistency. This cream will not make butter, but makes good ghee.

Keeping Milk Good.—Milk will keep good if a few points are carefully observed. China crockery retains heat and turns milk soon. The best kind of vessels to keep milk in are copper pans, from twelve to eighteen inches in length, seven inches wide and one and a half inch deep.

They should be well tinned, and before using should be well rubbed with dry wood ashes until every particle of grease is removed, then scalded with hot water and put in the sun to dry.

These pans should be placed side by side on a shelf and filled three-fourths with milk. The milk should be kept in a quiet room which is not used as a passage, and which can be shut up and kept cool. If people come in and out of the room they will disturb the atmosphere, and prevent the cream from properly forming. When the weather is warm the doors of the room should be opened out at night. The atmosphere of the room should be cool.

The cream vessel must not be moved or touched from the time it has been set to the moment of skimming.

Cold is favourable to the forming of cream; some people place their milk vessels in wet sand.

Changes in the weather affect milk very much; sometimes on a cloudy day the cream will be quite thin, and a fall in the barometer will soon sour the milk; milk and cream will lessen when a westerly wind blows; frost will prevent cream forming; a bright, clear, and calm day is most favourable. The wind can be shut out by closing the doors and windows. Should the milk turn sour any day, do not be discouraged, as it may be a storm is brewing, and the electricity in the air has turned the milk, or else the pan is dirty; when things go wrong look for the cause, and if possible remove it.

Skimmed Milk that has stood not longer than twelve hours is good, and may be used for all household purposes. If reboiled, skimmed milk will keep good for many hours; when milk has stood for more than twelve hours it should not be used for the table, but it will make good curd, or may be given to ducks, fowls, dogs, goats, and other animals. Skimmed milk, pure and undiluted, contains a great deal of nourishment, and produces muscle, and, as it is cheaper than pure unskimmed milk, should enter largely into man's daily food.

Boiling Milk.—In the hot weather and rains milk will not keep good for any length of time unless it is properly boiled. Boiled milk produces more cream than unboiled milk does. Milk intended for cream and butter should be boiled for a longer time than milk used for tea, coffee, and for children.

Susceptibility of Milk.—Milk, cream, and butter all take the flavour of any strong scent which may be near or about them. Milk while it is being boiled is sometimes turned sour by bad smells.

Silver and plated vessels and spoons will turn milk sour.

Iron turns it red and makes cream black, but does not make them sour.

Copper vessels, unless well tinned, will also turn milk sour; brass turns it green, and gives it a nasty flavour. When kept long in tin milk turns blue when put into tea.

Fresh earthen pots give milk, cream, and butter a strong and unpleasant earthy taste.

China is a retainer of heat, so that all milk jugs, cups, and basins are unsuited for keeping milk in.

Zinc, tinned copper, bell metal, and wood make the best milk vessels.

Vanilla has a wonderful effect in keeping milk sweet; a drop of its essence is a great help to keeping it good.

Milk carries infection; if milk is bought from the village or bazaar it should be well boiled before using, or else you may make up your mind that you may be infected with any disease prevailing in the bazaar or village.

CHAPTER XXIII.

BUTTER.

Boiled and unboiled Milk.—Until the thermometer rises to 70° butter may be made from cream of unboiled milk.

Butter thus made has, as some think, a finer flavour than butter made from cream of boiled milk; but boiled milk yields more cream and butter than unboiled milk does, and the longer milk is boiled the more cream and butter it yields.

If all the milk is used for butter, then set it for thirty-six hours in the cold weather and twenty-four hours in the warm weather; the cream then will collect into a thick paste, leaving the milk below quite thin and poor, unfit for household use, but good for fowls, ducks, goats, dogs, etc.

If the milk is to be used for butter as well as household purposes, it should not be allowed to stand for more than from twelve to sixteen hours in the cold weather, and an hour or two less in the hot weather.

It is more profitable to make butter of cream, and to let the milk stand for only twelve hours, as then the whole of the milk can be used for the household, and also a sufficient quantity of butter produced.

If the milk stands longer there will be more cream and butter, but the milk will be useless.

If there be more milk than is needed, then the surplus can be sold after it has been skimmed; skimmed milk will sell for from four to six pice a *seer*.

Collecting Cream.—When the cream is skimmed, collect it all in a large mug or bowl, until there is a large quantity. When two or three days' cream has been collected the butter may be made. Butter made from very fresh cream will often sour in a few hours. But by keeping the cream from twenty-four to forty-eight hours some chemical change takes place in it, by which the acid portion is separated from the greasy part, and the butter comes away more freely when churned.

The process of Butter-making is exceedingly simple. Butter made from cream must be made in an atmospheric churn. These churns can be had at European hardware shops.

Butter made from sour milk or tyer must be made in the native churn, in the native way. It will not yield much butter in an atmospheric churn.

The native Churn and mode of making butter are both very simple. This method of making butter produces a greater quantity of butter. The only objection is that all the milk is lost, as the whole of the milk turns sour. This sour butter-milk cannot be used for puddings, tea, etc., but, when fresh, it makes a very refreshing and nice drink, and is very cooling in the hot weather. It is much liked by natives and some Europeans.

The milk is boiled well, after which it is put into a large jar, and a teaspoonful of sour butter-milk or tyer is added to it, and it is put aside for twenty-four hours, when a quantity of *cold* water is added to it, and it is churned. From one to one and a half *chittack* of butter is produced from each *seer* of milk, if made by this method.

The churning apparatus consists of a stake some four feet long driven into the ground; to this, two feet apart from each other, are tied two rings made of cane or bamboo lathe. The jar containing the milk is placed at the foot of the stake under the rings, and the churn is passed through the two rings into the jar. Then a string is put round the churn between the two rings, and the churn is drilled for twenty minutes.

The churn is simply a piece of thin, smooth bamboo, five feet long, split into four at one end, and opened out to the width of three or four inches, with small pieces of bamboo placed crosswise to keep it open; this end is placed in the milk, and the churn is drilled.

The butter forms and floats in the jar, when it is

collected and cleaned and salted. Nearly all cooks and khansamas know how to make butter in this way.

The butter-milk will sell for from one to four pice a *seer*. Many people drink it, and also give it to their pigs, ducks, fowls, and dogs.

Atmospheric Churn.—By making butter in the atmospheric churn, you save nearly all the milk, though the quantity of butter is not great; by the native mode of making butter you can get from one to one and a half *chittack* of butter from every *seer* of milk; by making butter in the atmospheric churn with cream, you get only from half to three-fourths of a *chittack* of butter from the same quantity of milk, but the whole of the milk is good for use.

All the cream should be put into the churn, and a few mugs of *cold* water added. The water keeps the cream cool during the churning, and also being a harder fluid than milk, helps to beat up the butter. Commence churning slowly; the more slowly the butter comes the better it will be in both quality and quantity.

The churn must be securely closed. Care should be taken that the man does not hold the churn with his feet, or it will make it warm, and make the butter oily.

As soon as the fluid becomes heavy and cloggy, the churning should be done more slowly, and continued so until the churn runs easily again, and the sound of the fluid rattling about inside be distinguished; then the churner should look in to see if grains of butter are forming, and continue churning gently until the butter forms a solid lump in the churn.

If the butter is turned out before it has formed a solid lump a great deal is lost, as it is impossible to collect all the frothy particles when it has once been taken out of the churn. Servants, if not watched, will always take it out too soon.

When the butter is ready, pour off the butter-milk, and give it to the cows, calves, goats, dogs, and fowls. Wash the butter with *cold* water which has been standing all night in an earthen *soric* or *ghurra*; fresh water from the well or tank or tap is sure to be warm, and will make the butter soft. After washing it thoroughly, it should be salted and made into pats, and put into an earthen pot filled with *cold* water; butter made in this way will keep sweet and nice for many days; it should be rewashed and salted every morning until the next churning day.

Butter should never be touched with the hand or left in a warm place for even a few seconds. A wooden or bamboo spoon and knife should be used. The churning should always be done early in the morning.

After the thermometer reaches 70°, butter-making becomes troublesome, as the heat makes it soft and oily.

Pieces of ice should be dropped into the churn while churning to harden the butter, and the churn should be placed in a tub of *cold* water.

Cleanliness.—Want of perfect cleanliness is a great obstacle to successful butter-making, especially so in the hot weather; and without the eye of the housekeeper perfect cleanliness is not to be obtained in this country, where most of the people do not know a clean thing from a dirty one. The least dirt will spoil the whole of the butter. The same spoon that has been used to skim the morning's milk should not be used to skim the evening's milk. All the vessels and implements should be kept perfectly clean, and soaked in clean water until the time they are needed for use. Deal and bamboo are the only kinds of wood that should be used in butter-making.

Preserving Butter.—After churning, wash and salt the butter, and keep it in an earthen (*mutti*) vessel full of cold water, in a cool place; the water must be changed morning and evening. The ice-box is a good place to keep butter in.

Sweet or Sour Cream.—"Sweet cream is not the best for making butter, as it yields less than cream that is slightly sour. The best and most butter is made from cream that is slightly sour, and which is taken from milk set in shallow pans in a room not over sixty or sixty-two degrees of temperature for thirty-six hours, then skimmed and kept twenty-four hours at the same temperature before churning, and churned at this same temperature. When cream is too sour or is too warm, it will foam in the churn and give out a large quantity of carbonic acid gas. This interferes with the making of the butter. It will not do this otherwise. To bring the cream, when thus disturbed, into proper condition, add cold water to thin it, by which the gas evolved in the churning escapes and the foaming is reduced. Then the butter separates. This foaming is a common thing in the summer, while in the winter, owing to the cold, the cream granulates and appears to be sandy, and the butter does not come. The remedy then is to add warm water to the cream, as it is too cold, and the fine grains of butter will not adhere together."—*American Farmer.*

CHAPTER XXIV.

GHEE.

Making Ghee.—Collect all your spare butter of the last few days, and put it into a small *deghchee* on a clear charcoal fire, *not too hot*, and let it boil gently. Always have it done in your presence in some convenient spot. At first it will froth up like whipped cream, then by degrees it will curdle, and small white opaque particles will be observed inside; after a time the particles will begin to adhere to the bottom of the *deghchee*, leaving the *ghee* quite clear; when it is nearly ready it will leave off frothing and will simmer quietly, rising in round glossy bubbles; now stir gently with a spoon, so that the froth at the top may go down, but do not disturb what has caked at the bottom, which after a time will look like a poached egg; while all above will look like salad oil, clear and bright. It is now done. Take it off the fire and pour it gently into an empty bottle with a large mouth, and, when cool, cork down tightly and cover the cork with bees-wax, sealing-wax, or bladder which has been soaked in bluestone and water, otherwise the ants will eat off the cork and bladder.

As the *ghee* cools, it will look like good honey. If carefully made it will keep good for years.

The great secret in making *ghee* is patience. It must not be boiled on too hot a fire or it will burn, turn brown, and smell nasty.

Home-made *ghee* when used for cooking is just as nice and wholesome as butter, but the bazaar *ghee* is nasty, adulterated stuff.

Clarifying Ghee.—If *ghee* has been kept any time, and there is a doubt about its sweetness, or if *ghee* has been bought from the bazaar or village, it should be turned into a *deghchee* or saucepan, and reboiled. Put a cupful of milk, a teaspoonful of salt, and a few cloves and lemon leaves into it before putting it on the fire. It will become as fresh and sweet and clear as newly made *ghee*.

CHAPTER XXV.

CURD, CHEESE, AND TYER.

Curd is a very useful article of food, and makes many delicious dishes for the table. It enters very largely into the diet of the people of India, and in some places sells as high as 1½ to 2 *seers* for the rupee.

Making Curd.—Curd is made from fresh milk or skimmed milk. Sometimes skimmed milk turns in the boiling of itself, if put on a quick fire; but fresh milk will not turn unless something is put into it.

Put the milk into a *deghchee* or saucepan, and put it over the fire; let it boil up, then put a dessertspoonful of butter into it and stir well, or put a cupful of whey, or half a cupful of sour butter-milk or tyer, or a little lemon juice, and keep stirring. In a little while the curd will form and separate from the whey.

If you want fine, soft curd, drain off the whey while it is hot and use the curd immediately.

But if large-grained hard curd is required, then let it cool before draining off the whey; put it in a piece of clean cloth, tie tightly, and hang it up and let the last drop of whey drain off. This will give you a nice cake of curd. Unskimmed milk produces better curd than skimmed milk does.

Cream Cheese.—Cream cheese is best when made from curds of fresh unboiled milk. The process of making it is very simple. Turn the milk, put the curds into a clean cloth, and let the whey drain off. Open the cloth, remove the curd, place it in a plate or dish, add salt to taste and thoroughly mix; then put into a clean cloth, carefully fold the cloth over it, and place it on a piece of board under a good weight till the remaining whey is drained off. When this is done it is ready for use. Cream cheese is very good when fresh, but it will not be nearly as nice if kept long.

Tyer.—The native name for tyer is *duhhee.* It is made thus:—Take a *seer* or two of pure, fresh milk, boil on a slow fire until it is boiled down to half or two-thirds of the quantity. Pour it into a large-mouthed shallow dish; an earthen (*mutti*) dish is preferable. Put half a cupful of tyer into it, and place it in a quiet, cool corner and let it stand for twelve hours, when it will be ready for use.

CHAPTER XXVI.

LICE, TICKS, FLIES, ETC.

Lice.—Cattle must be kept perfectly free from all kinds of vermin. When their coats are long, especially in the winter, cattle are troubled much by lice of a bluish colour, and very small. If these are not immediately removed, the cow will get quite sickly from the great irritation. The cure is simple: rub Phenyle and water or Keating's insect powder well over the animal. The insects are so small that they will escape detection unless the coat is carefully examined. When you observe a cow rubbing herself constantly, look for parasites.

Calves often get them in large numbers, and if neglected become very weak and die.

Dog-ticks also attack cows. Ticks must be carefully picked off. They cling about the udder, and under the elbows of the poor creatures, in places where they can neither be scratched nor rubbed off, and a cow will often put down her head and sigh with relief when they are removed.

After the ticks have been removed some Phenyle and water should be rubbed over the animal; one to twenty parts of water should be used.

Flies trouble cattle very much. The gad-fly bites very severely, also the common house-fly will get in under the hair of the cow and worry her. If cattle are properly groomed and kept thoroughly clean, and occasionally washed with a weak solution of Phenyle, they will not be troubled very much with flies.

Mosquitoes also plague cattle very much. The cattle-house must be properly smoked every evening. Burn some refuse straw and dried cow-dung at the door of the house windward on a slow fire. This will drive the mosquitoes away.

Throw a little incense or ground sulphur on the fire.

A good cure for lice, ticks, etc., is:—

Mustard-oil	8 chittacks
Spirits of turpentine	4 chittacks
Gum camphor	2 chittacks
Ground sulphur	4 chittacks
Phenyle	1 chittack

well mixed and rubbed over the animal. Care must be taken not to allow the stuff to get into the eye.

CHAPTER XXVII.

THE SEASONS OF THE YEAR.

It may be said that in India the year is divided into three seasons, the cold, the hot, and the rains.

The cold weather lasts from the 15th of October to the 1st of March. At this season cattle need more nourishing food, and a greater quantity of it, than in the hot weather. At night they should be always covered with a blanket or a warm coat especially made for them.

Keeping cattle out of doors in the sun during the day, except from 12 to 2, at this season, does them good, but they must be protected from the sharp, cold winds and rain, and always be placed in a warm house during the night. The milk-cow feels the cold very much, and her milk is affected by it.

There will be sufficient grass on properly managed lands for the cattle at this season. From the end of September to the beginning of March, a good stock of hay, *bhoosa* (chaff), and straw must be stored up for the cattle to feed on from the 1st of March to the 15th of July, when grass and straw will be scarce. If this is not done the cattle will suffer and become diseased. From October to March you can get grain and chaff cheap, and it is advisable to buy then and store away for use during the year. In February, wheat, kullie, and other chaff can be obtained in abundance.

The hot weather begins from the 1st of March, and ends the 15th of June to the 1st of July. At this season cattle suffer much from want of food, and, if not cared for, will die; but they will keep in better condition on the same quantity that they got in the cold weather. The midday sun is injurious, but all cattle may be tied out of doors at night with advantage. A close stall will lessen the milk of a cow.

At this season there will not be much green food for the cattle, and they must be given an abundant supply of hay and *bhoosa* (chaff) during the day and at night.

Tender green leaves also are very good for them. It is best to grow some special green food for the cattle at this season.

The rains begin from the 15th of June to the 1st of July, and end by the 15th of October.

At this season there is an abundant supply of grass and other green food for the cattle. .

Cattle will not suffer any ill from drizzles or light showers of rain; but great care must be taken that they are not exposed to heavy rains and storms, or put into their stalls at night while they are wet. Servants must be constantly watched, otherwise they will leave the cow-house dirty and wet, and this will be very injurious to the cattle.

Cattle should never be tied out at night during this season, and should be carefully protected from all storms and cold winds.

Cattle may be let out during the day at all seasons, and they will not suffer any inconvenience, if only they are protected from the midday sun, storms, heavy rains, cold cutting winds, and damp. They must not be allowed to graze on marshy grounds, or lands that are not properly drained.

Great care must be exercised at all seasons to guard the cattle against contagion. The farther they are kept from the roads and the village cattle the better.

CHAPTER XXVIII.

CATTLE-DUNG.

Cattle-Dung is largely used by natives as fuel, and for plastering their houses; some use it for manure. The last-named is its legitimate use, and if the natives would not burn it up, but use it for manuring their lands, they would get better harvests, and would be able to afford to burn wood and coal, which would be more conducive to health. The commoner classes of natives who have cows never buy wood or coal for fuel; they make dung-cakes or rolls, and dry them, and cook their food with them. Often they have more than they need for their own use, so they sell the surplus to those who have none.

Profit.—The dung, when it is fresh, can be sold, or made into cakes or rolls for fuel, or it can be turned into manure and sold. A properly fed cow will produce at least a pice worth of dung every day.

Manure-pits.—For making manure a pit four feet square or larger, according to the number of cattle, should be dug, and all the dung and refuse foods thrown into it every morning and evening. When the pit is nearly full, a lot of water should be poured over the heap to make the stuff moist, and then it should be covered over with a foot and a half or two feet of dry earth. The pit must be kept closed for six months; after that the manure will be fit for use.

These pits should be a good distance away from the dwelling-house, and not only far from but below the water-level of the tank or well. Great care must be taken to properly cover the pits; any negligence in this matter may cause much sickness and loss.

CHAPTER XXIX.

GRASS-LAND.

Providing Fodder for cattle in India is a subject deserving the most serious and careful consideration of all zemindars and the Government of India.

The ryots in India do not feel the necessity for providing pasture-lands, and leave their cattle, to die for want of food. The cattle are left to browse on the roadsides, or are tied near their house to only gaze at the fields of paddy and wheat around them. No special food is provided for them. The consequence is that the cattle are only skin and bones, and so weak and stunted that they are unable to do much work. Besides, a great number die every year, and the ryots are unable to cultivate their lands. The result is, ryots are not able to pay their rents, or have sufficient food for their families. Every village should be compelled to have grass-lands for its cattle.

There should be a law compelling the zemindars and ryots to reserve land in every village for grazing cattle. One *biggah* per head of cattle should be the minimum allowed. If there be 200 head of cattle in a village, there should be 200 *biggahs* of grazing land reserved in this village. Each cattle owner should be compelled to reserve as many *biggahs* of land for grazing as the number of cattle he has. The zemindar should take a nominal rent for this land, and the cattle owner should be punished if he cultivates this land or uses it for any purpose other than grazing cattle. The Magistrate of the district should select the land to be thus reserved in each village. This he could easily do personally, or through his assistants and deputies when on tour.

Europeans and the richer class of natives buy fodder for their cattle, and do not let them starve or suffer. But buying grass and green food is very expensive.

If you have a piece of land that you can set apart for grass, you will do wisely if you cultivate fodder. It will be cheaper than buying fodder, and your cows will be sure to have green food all the year round.

Amount of Land needed.—Three and a half *biggahs* or one acre of land will be sufficient to provide green food for one cow. For village cattle even one *biggah* per head will suffice to keep them alive, but good cows cannot thrive on less than three and a half *biggahs*. In dairy-farms, where the cows consume large quantities of food, it will require two acres or seven *biggahs* to supply a cow with all the food she needs. A *biggah* is 14,400 square feet, or 120 feet by 120 feet.

Some say it is best to grow grain on the land, and stall-feed the cattle. Others, again, say it is more profitable to grow only grass and hay, for then the cattle will have a greater abundance of food and will thrive better. My opinion is, that of the seven *biggahs*, two and a half ought to be left in grass, and barley, kullie, or wheat should be grown on the remaining five *biggahs*. This will give the animal sufficient grass, grain, chaff, and bran during the year.

Fertility of the Land.—Pasture-lands need proper management. Many persons graze their cattle on the land from January to December, or cut away the grass, and never think of doing anything to improve the lands. They think grass-lands need no care or management. But this is a serious mistake. The very best land could not long bear this strain upon its productive powers.

There are two ways of retaining the fertility of land; either by the application of manure, or by frequent stirring up of the soil. Proper and regular irrigation is another plan for improving the grass-land. In some parts of India there is to be found some water which runs to waste, but could be turned to account during the hot weather, for the improvement of the grass-land, if only a little ingenuity were exercised. But in most places water is very scarce in the hot weather, and it would be a great expense to irrigate the land. The best and easiest method is to manure the land every year.

The best time to manure the land is March, when the land is almost bare ; the March showers will speedily wash it down to the roots of the grass.

Preparation of Land.—Before the manure is put down on the ground, all the jungle and coarse patches of grass must be taken up by the roots. The enormous strain made upon the land by all this jungle and coarse grass renders their extermination necessary. After this, the land should be well ploughed and harrowed, then the manure should be put over the land, and the plough and harrow drawn over it again, and the stones picked up. After the harrowing, the land should be properly levelled and rolled. The ploughing is necessary only for the first manuring ; the second year the land should be well weeded and rolled, and the manure put down, and the harrow passed over it ; after this, the stones should be picked up. Every five years the land should be thoroughly ploughed. The best manure is procured from the cow-house.

Draining.—Grass-lands must be properly drained, and should the drains become faulty, they must be repaired.

Unless the lands are well drained the grass will be stunted and destroyed.

If the lands are properly manured and drained, there will be an abundant supply of grass all through the year.

Doob is the best grass to grow. If you find the grass on the land is coarse and of an unnutritious kind, then thoroughly plough up the whole land, and manure well, and sow the *doob*. The *doob* is very nice and soft, and very nutritious, and all cattle, goats, and sheep eat it very greedily. The seed of the *doob* can be obtained from any of the gardens. If the seed is not obtainable, take up a lot of the grass by the root, and cut it up into pieces one inch long, and scatter it over the land, and put the harrow over it. Guinea grass is also very good for cattle.

Lucern grass or clover is bad for cows in India, as it heats the blood and dries up the milk, and makes the animal want to calve long before the ordinary time. It may be given to bulls, bullocks, and horses, and also to young heifers if you want them to calve early; but as it tries a cow's constitution if she calves too young, and the calf is likely to be weakly, it is better not to hurry nature.

Green Food.—Wheat, barley, kullia or woorid and Indian corn, when they are green and very young, make splendid food for cattle, and make the cow's milk very rich.

WEIGHTS AND MEASURES.

Measures of Capacity.

1 Minim (♏.)	=	1 Drop.
1 Dram	=	1 Teaspoonful—$\frac{1}{16}$ Chittack.
2 Drams	=	1 Dessertspoonful—$\frac{1}{8}$ Chittack.
4 Drams	=	1 Tablespoonful—$\frac{1}{4}$ Chittack.
60 Minims (♏.)	=	1 Dram (ʒ)—$\frac{1}{16}$ Chittack.
8 Drams	=	1 Ounce (℥)—$\frac{1}{2}$ Chittack.
20 Ounces	=	1 Pint—10 Chittacks.
4 Gills	=	1 Pint—10 Chittacks.
2 Pints	=	1 Quart—$1\frac{1}{4}$ Seer.
2 Quarts	=	1 Pottle—$2\frac{1}{2}$ Seers.
4 Quarts	=	1 Gallon—5 Seers.
2 Gallons	=	1 Peck—10 Seers.
4 Pecks	=	1 Bushel—1 Maund.
2 Bushels	=	1 Strike—2 Maunds.
3 Bushels	=	1 Sack—3 Maunds.
8 Bushels	=	1 Quarter—8 Maunds.
12 Sacks	=	1 Chaldron—36 Maunds.
5 Quarters	=	1 Wey or Load—40 Maunds.
10 Quarters	=	1 Last—80 Maunds.

Avoirdupois Weight.

16 Drams	=	1 Ounce ($437\frac{1}{2}$ grains)—$\frac{1}{2}$ Chittack.
16 Ounces	=	1 Pound (lb.)—$\frac{1}{2}$ Seer.
14 Pounds	=	1 Stone—7 Seers.
28 Pounds	=	1 Quarter—14 Seers.
112 Pounds	=	1 Hundredwt. (cwt.)—1 Maund, 16 Seers.
20 Hundredweights	=	1 Ton—28 Maunds.

Square and Land Measure.

144 Inches	=	1 Square Foot.
9 Feet	=	1 Square Yard.
$30\frac{1}{4}$ Yards	=	1 Square Rod.
16 Poles	=	1 Chain.
40 Poles	=	1 Rood.
4 Roods	=	1 Acre (4840 yards).
640 Acres	=	1 Square Mile.

BAZAAR WEIGHT.

4 Sicki . . .	=	1 Tola—1 rupee.
5 Sicki . . .	=	1 Kutcha—1¼ rupee weight.
4 Kutchas. . .	=	1 Chittack—5 rupees weight.
4 Chittacks . .	=	1 Powah—20 rupees weight.
4 Powahs . . .	=	1 Seer—80 rupees weight.
5 Seers . . .	=	1 Pusseree—10 lbs. or 10 lbs. 10 oz.
8 Pusserees . .	=	1 Maund—80 or 82½ lbs.

Four bundles of straw or hay make one Gonda.

20 Gondas . . .	=	1 Pon.
16 Pons . . .	=	1 Kahon.

Bengal Square or Land Measure.

5 Haths loug × 4 Broad = 1 Chittack.

1 Chittack	=		45 sq. ft.	or	5 sq. yds.	
16 Chittacks	=	1 Cottah =	720	,, or	80	,,
20 Cottahs	=	1 Bigha =	14,400	,, or	1600	,,

3½ Bighas = 1 Acre.

CHAPTER XXX.

DAIRY-FARMING.

I HAVE often heard it said, it is impossible for a European in this country to make a living by dairy-farming; and I am told of several persons who have sunk large sums of money in the attempt. On inquiry I find these persons failed because they had no knowledge whatever of the business, and went about the whole thing in a way that certainly could not ensure success. Some people seem to think all they have to do to work a dairy is to buy a few cows and employ some gowallahs to feed and milk the cows and sell the milk. They know nothing about cows, so they get their servants to buy them; they know nothing about feeding cattle, so they allow their servants to give the cows whatever they please; they know nothing about the care of cattle, so the cows are not cared for properly; they know nothing about milk and butter-making, so these things are entrusted to the servants, and the milk and butter may contain anything. These people start with a great noise and flourish, and induce some of their friends and neighbours to patronise them, but in a short time they are unable to supply what they agree to supply, and what they do supply is of doubtful quality, so in a little while their customers, one after another, withdraw and go back to natives, or try to find a more reliable source of supply. The cost of servants and food for the cows exceeds the receipts for milk and butter produced, and the poor dairyman finds himself in debt if not bankrupt, and in six months or a year the business is closed. This is the disastrous experience of most of the Europeans who have tried to dairy-farm in this country. Now anyone with any sense will see that people of this type will never succeed in dairy-farming.

There are certain things necessary in dairy-farming, and without these essentials it is impossible for anyone to succeed in the business. First, the person—be it man or woman—must have some practical knowledge of the business. That is, he must serve an apprenticeship of at least one year in some properly conducted large dairy before he can work one himself. Second, he must be diligent and prepared to do a large portion of the work himself. He must know what to do and when and how to do it, and must order and supervise every detail of the work personally, and not allow any servant to manage or interfere with the business. The servants must be under absolute control. Third, he must be absolutely honest, and not allow any of his servants to do anything that he himself would not do. He must do all he can to merit the confidence the people have placed in him in taking his milk and butter. Fourth, he must be able to supply the demand for milk and butter as the demand daily increases. If, even for a short time, he is unable to do so, those whom he has failed to supply will seek other sources for their supply, and he will probably lose their custom permanently.

As I have said above, the four things essential to dairy-farming are, knowledge, diligence, honesty, and capital; without these four combined no one can possibly succeed for any length of time.

India is certainly one of the best countries for dairy-farming. Land and food stuff are cheap, labour is cheap, cattle are cheap, and the milk of the Indian cow is just as rich as the richest milk produced in England and America. Most of the cows in India are equal to the Jersey cow for richness of milk. Then again, milk and butter bring higher prices in India than in England and America.

A few figures here will be interesting. In England it takes from two and a half to four gallons, or twenty-five to forty pounds, of milk to make one pound of butter. In India it takes from twelve to twenty-four pounds of milk to make one pound of butter. In England good butter fetches from one shilling to one shilling and twopence a pound; in America the same butter will sell for from twelve to twenty cents a pound; and in India it will bring from one rupee to one rupee four annas a pound. Then again, in England fresh milk sells for from eightpence to one shilling a gallon; in America such milk will fetch from twelve to twenty cents a gallon; and in India you will get from thirteen annas to a rupee for a gallon of pure fresh milk.

It costs less to produce milk and butter in India than it does in either England or America, and milk and butter sell for higher prices in India than they do either in England or America. Now if the above-mentioned facts prove anything, they prove that it is quite possible to successfully work a dairy-farm in India.

EXPERIENCE.—I would advise any person wishing to start a dairy-farm to first spend a year in one of the first-class dairy-farms in England or India, or in one of the Government dairies, and study every detail of the work. Some private dairies can be conducted successfully by studying books and buying knowledge from daily experience, but for dairy-farming on a large scale a practical knowledge of the business is absolutely necessary to start with.

CAPITAL.—To make a dairy-farm pay enough to enable a man to comfortably support a family, it must be worked on a large scale. From fifty to a hundred cows must be kept. The outlay for cattle, lands, buildings, utensils, implements, etc., will be between thirty and forty thousand rupees. A small dairy with thirty cows will cost between ten and fifteen thousand rupees. The outlay could be considerably reduced by renting lands and houses instead of buying and building. But the high rents will take away a great deal from the profits.

THE POSITION OF THE DAIRY-FARM.—The dairy should be situated in the suburbs of a city or town, or near a city or town, close to a railway station. The milk and butter must be delivered at regular hours to the consumers; the usual times are between five and six o'clock in the morning and four and five o'clock in the evening, and unless the dairy is so situated that this can be done conveniently and at a small cost, it will be impossible to conduct the business successfully.

The position of the dairy must be elevated above the surrounding land, so as to give a natural drainage. The ground must be perfectly dry, and even during the heaviest rain no water must lodge on any part of it. Attached to the farm building or immediately adjoining it there should be a large tract of land for grazing the dry cows and the calves, and for letting out milk-cows for exercise. There should be two acres or seven *biggahs* of land for each cow. A dairy with one hundred cows will need two hundred acres of land. If it is impossible to obtain all this immediately near the farm building, there must be sufficient land near it to enable the milk-cows and little calves to exercise, and the grazing lands may be situated farther away.

The land should be divided into different lots. A third should be allowed the cattle for grazing and exercise, and two-thirds cultivated and sown under barley, wheat, or kullie for cattle food. There should be large trees on the land to give shade to the cattle.

THE CLASS OF CATTLE NEEDED.—The success of a dairy depends in a large measure upon the cows in the dairy. If the cows are bad milkers they will eat much and yield little. The dairyman must procure and produce the best milkers. By best milkers, I mean cows that will give the largest quantity of milk, containing the largest quantity of butter-fat. No cow giving less than 3600 lbs. of milk, yielding 180 lbs. of butter, in ten months, is worth keeping in a dairy. A cow that gives ten *seers* of milk and one and a quarter pound of butter a day is a good cow. Some cows will yield from twelve to fourteen *seers* of milk a day and produce one and a half to two and a quarter pounds of butter. Some cows will milk for ten or twelve months, others again will yield only for six or eight months. It is always more profitable to have the best. It is a "penny-wise pound-foolish" policy to buy cheap cows that will yield little milk, and that for only six or eight months.

The dairyman must select his cattle with the greatest

care, for his success or failure will depend upon these cattle. Good cows will be found among every breed; some cross-bred cows are very good milkers. By cross-breds I mean crosses between pure Hissar, Nellore, Nagouri, Goorgaira, Guzerati, Sindi, or English cattle, and not between the better breeds and the common village cattle. I would advise dairymen to select their cows from among the following pure breeds—Hissar, Nellore, Goorgaira, Guzerati, Sindi, or crosses between the English cow and bulls of the above-mentioned pure Indian breeds.

Dry Cows.—It will always be found more satisfactory to keep the best cows after they become dry than to sell them to the butchers. If the cows are properly managed they will milk for three or four months after calving, and then take the bull. They will continue to give milk for six months after taking the bull, then remain dry three or four months, when they will come into the dairy again in perfect condition. I have treated this subject more fully in a previous chapter.

Breeding for the Dairy.—It is more profitable for a dairyman to breed his own cows than to buy them. If the dairy is properly managed and there are good grass-lands this can easily be done at a small cost. *See the chapter on breeding.*

Bulls.—Every dairy should have a couple of really

first-class Hissar or Nellore bulls to serve the cows as they come into season. Unless this is done the cows will become permanently spoiled. *See previous chapter on this subject.*

IMPORTANT MATTERS.—I have already written about the mode of feeding cattle, the need of exercise, cleanliness, regularity, kindness to the cows and calves, rearing calves, etc., and I will refer the reader to those chapters for information.

BUFFALOES.—Most of the dairies in India keep large numbers of buffaloes for milk. The better breeds of buffaloes give large quantities of milk; some have given from five to eight gallons, that is, fifty to eighty pounds a day. The milk is much richer than cow's milk. It usually takes eight to twelve pounds of this milk to make one pound of butter. Buffaloes are very large and gross eaters; they will consume three times the quantity of food a cow will consume. Buffaloes are more delicate than cows, and succumb to disease much more quickly. The buffalo-calf is more difficult to rear than the cow's calf.

I consider buffaloes to be altogether unsuitable for dairy purposes. My chief reasons for coming to this conclusion are, first, the milk of the buffalo is very heating and unfit for human consumption until it is first skimmed and largely diluted with water. It may prove less injurious in the hills and colder climates, but is absolutely harmful in the plains. Parents who have the welfare of their children at heart should never allow them to have buffalo-milk. If this milk is given to children they will suffer from liver, bowel, and other complaints caused by biliousness and over-heating of the blood. Mr. H. A. Howman in his report on dairy work in India, submitted to Government in 1890, fully corroborates my statements. He says buffalo-milk is very likely to act prejudicially on the liver of both children and invalids. He found that buffalo-milk was used in the Scottish Orphanage at Bombay, and this milk often made the children ill. Unscrupulous dairy-men sell buffalo-milk for cow's milk, or mix the two together and send it out as pure cow's milk.

It is a most significant fact that experienced native horse-breeders in India will not give buffalo-milk to young horses, because, as they say, horses reared on buffalo-milk succumb to heat and fatigue much sooner than horses reared on cow's milk.

The natives make tyer and ghee from buffalo-milk, but very few, except the hill tribes and people of the colder parts of India, will drink the milk itself. Buffalo-milk is considered very much inferior to cow's milk, and if cow's milk sells at six *seers* for the rupee, buffalo-milk will sell at nine *seers*.

Second, the butter made from buffalo-milk is not nearly as good as butter made from cow's milk. Buffalo-butter is very white, and has not the nice flavour of cow's butter. To remedy this a lot of colouring and flavouring has to be used; but notwithstanding all the doctoring this butter has to undergo, it is very inferior to butter made from pure cow's milk. The only thing it is good for is ghee. If butter were made from unadulterated buffalo-milk and then turned into ghee, it would serve a useful purpose, but most of the buffalo-milk and ghee you get from the natives is adulterated with a stuff called "tree tallow," and also with certain oils. The better class of natives have a strong objection to ghee made from buffalo-milk. If "Gowah ghee," or ghee made from cow's milk, will sell at one *seer* for the rupee, "Moashar ghee"—ghee from buffalo-milk—will sell at one and a half to two *seers* for the rupee.

No dairyman can afford to make ghee for sale. It will take about one and a quarter to one and a half pound of butter to make one pound of ghee, and ghee sells at from two to three pounds for the rupee. The dairyman should let buffaloes alone, and confine his operations to cows only.

SOME DIFFICULTIES.—The dairyman must not think that all before him will be smooth sailing. He may by proper care and watchfulness keep disease away from his cattle; he may by proper selections and good management make his cows yield large profits; he may by fair dealing and punctuality gain a large constituency; but he will have to fight for the victory. The chief enemies are the native servants. His own servants will lie, steal, neglect the cattle, shirk their duty, and give no end of trouble. He can never trust a single man so as to depend upon him absolutely. He must watch them closely, and stand over them in everything they do; otherwise they will soon defeat him and cause endless loss. The servants will be in league with the people outside The man who supplies the oilcake, grain, chaff, or straw will find it to his advantage to give the servants a certain percentage on the amounts consumed, so that the consumption will increase; and it will be to the servants' advantage to run up the food-supply bills as much as possible, and if they cannot do this they will steal the food stuff and starve the cattle. It will be to the chamar's advantage to give the servants so much for each skin he can get, and the master will wonder why his cattle are dying, never suspecting that the good Hindoos have poisoned his cows and calves. It will also be to the advantage of the native milkman to get this dairy out of his way; so he takes the servants on the dairy-farm into his confidence and service to gain his purpose, and the dairyman will find his cows do not yield the milk or butter they should. Then again, there are the servants of the consumers. They want *dustoori* or bribes. If it is not given, the milk is tampered with and no end of complaints are received:

and then, in a great many cases, the milk is rejected. Finally, there are the ignorant and senseless masters and mistresses who are controlled by their servants and will believe all and do all their rascally servants tell them. These are the chief trials and difficulties in the way of the dairyman. If he can surmount these, his success is assured.

BOOK II.

CHAPTER I.

DISEASES OF CATTLE, GOATS, AND SHEEP.

MR. HALLEN says,—There are many diseases of a very serious type that cattle are subject to. Some of them are very contagious and most fatal.

These diseases are commonly met with in India, and unless proper preventive and curative measures are promptly adopted on the appearance of any contagious disease in the district or in the herd, you must not be surprised if most of your cattle are attacked and destroyed by it.

Cattle, when properly cared for and fed, seldom become ill.

When they are over-fed or badly fed, they become unhealthy and suffer much from disease.

Some of the diseases are contracted from contagion, while others are solely attributable to mismanagement in the care and feeding.

The causes of the different diseases are herein fully explained; and in most cases the causes can be prevented by ordinary care and watchfulness, so cattle owners will have only themselves to blame if any of these diseases attack their stock.

Hay, straw, *bhoosa*, bran, etc., must be stored for seasons of drought, inundation, heavy rains, or when cattle plague may be prevailing. Generally, cattle are let loose to pick up what they can as food; and very often they eat acrid or poisonous plants and grass. In India, after the inundation subsides, the submerged pastures are very injurious and cause disease.

If cattle are sent out to graze during the rains, great care must be taken that the lands are properly drained.

Cattle cannot remain healthy if exposed to heavy rains or kept on inundated lands, or are not sheltered from the heat of the midday sun, and cold, damp winds at night.

Disease is very often caused from the foul water the cattle are allowed to drink.

Rinderpest is the most contagious disease among cattle in India, and is very fatal. From 50 to 90 per cent. of the cattle attacked die.

Black-quarter, gloss-anthrax, and splenic apoplexy in cattle and braxy in sheep are undoubtedly contagious in India, and very fatal; an animal seldom recovers. Braxy in sheep is, however, rarely met with in India.

The following rules should be strictly adhered to :—

I. When cattle, sheep, or goats are purchased at a fair they should be always treated as having been exposed to contagion, as cattle and sheep are brought to the fair from all directions, and in one direction or other rinderpest or foot and mouth disease, or both diseases, very probably have lately been or are prevailing.

II. When cattle, sheep, or goats are being moved from one locality to another, they should not be allowed to mix with others *en route*, and should never be kept at night in or near any *serai* or bazaar, as a *serai* is often contaminated by being occupied, or having lately been occupied, by diseased animals; they should travel in the cool time of the day—this should be particularly observed during the hot weather; and they ought not to travel more than eight or ten miles during the twenty-four hours. They should be frequently watered and well fed.

III. When cattle, sheep, or goats are purchased in a fair or elsewhere, they should, on being brought to the purchaser's premises, be kept by themselves and not allowed to mix with the old cattle of the farm at pasture or watering time, or at any time. They should be kept by themselves for at least one to three months, in order to have proof whether they are affected with disease or not.

During that time the newly purchased animals should be carefully inspected morning and evening, and if any contagion appears among them, the affected animals should be at once isolated, and the remainder separated into small lots and picketed at some distance apart. At the end of three months, if no disease has appeared among them, they may be safely pastured and kept with the other cattle.

IV. When cattle are travelling, or are moved from one district to another, they are exposed to contagion and are liable to contract disease; therefore on their arrival at home they should be carefully examined, and if they have passed through an infected district, they should be kept by themselves for some time.

V. When disease, supposed to be of a contagious nature, appears among cattle, sheep, or goats, the first important duty is to separate the sick from the healthy animals.

VI. Carefully examine all the animals, and remove to the hospital any showing the slightest symptoms of disease.

VII. During the prevalence of contagion, divide the healthy cattle into several lots, making each lot as small in number as space will permit. Picket the cattle in such lots a good distance apart, and to windward of the sick cattle. Frequently examine each lot, and remove at once any animal in the least unwell. By steadily adopting this plan, the disease will be found in a few days to exist only among one or two lots, and by at once removing to the hospital any becoming sick, the disease will speedily be arrested in spreading through the herd. Each lot should be kept isolated from other cattle for about two or three months after being put by themselves, or after the last animal of the lot affected has been removed.

VIII. The hospital should be at a good distance from the cow-shed, enclosed by a strong fence. The attendants and the sick cattle must not be permitted to leave the enclosure. Food and water may be taken to the attendants and cattle, but no forage or water, litter, or clothing, or anything should be taken from the hospital. Dogs should not be allowed to go to and from the hospital, as they will carry contagion.

IX. The dry litter, etc., of the hospital should be burnt inside the hospital area, and the moist dung and discharges, etc., should be frequently removed from the stalls, and buried in pits dug in the hospital premises. These pits should be six feet or more deep, and should be filled with the wet litter, dung, etc., of the hospital up to within two feet of the surrounding ground surface, and then quicklime and good fresh earth should be used to fill up the remaining two feet.

X. The stalls, walls, etc., and ground of the hospital should be scrupulously cleaned by frequent sweeping and washing, and after every cleansing, McDougall's disinfecting powder, or Phenyle, lime, good ashes, or even dry earth, should be plentifully scattered over the floors and ground, and the woodwork and walls should be first washed and then whitewashed with lime and catechu.

XI. The hospital should be well ventilated. Sulphur fumigation should be daily carried out for an hour or so in the hospital building; and at this time the doors and windows should be closed, and the ventilators only kept partly open.

XII. The sick cattle should be kept scrupulously clean, and have thin rice, wheat, and corn gruel, and fresh green grass as diet. The healthy cattle should also be kept on soft and laxative food, as cattle fed on hard dry food have the disease in a more severe form than those fed on laxative fodder.

XIII. When these contagious diseases have prevailed among cattle or sheep, they should not be allowed to pasture or be kept with unaffected herds until three months have expired after the last case of disease occurring among the affected lot.

XIV. Animals that recover should be well washed with warm water and soap prior to being removed from the hospital. Phenyle should be added to the warm water, in the proportion of one wineglassful to a gallon of water.

XV. Carcases of stock that die of rinderpest, black-quarter, and other forms of anthrax fever, pleuro-pneumonia and foot-and-mouth disease, should be buried and covered with at least four feet of earth.

XVI. The hides of cattle that die of these contagious

diseases should be well scored and slashed with a knife, and buried with the carcases.

XVII. The surface of earth floors of stalls and ground on which cattle affected with contagious disease have been kept, should be removed and buried, and the earth below should be well dug up and turned over and the floor remade with fresh earth. Brick and stone floors may be scraped, washed, and disinfected with quicklime or carbolic acid.

XVIII. Poles of carts and harness, or saddlery, etc., used by animals affected with contagious disease, should be washed and disinfected. The old lining and stuffing of pack-saddles, etc., should be removed and burnt.

XIX. Half doses of medicine for calves, goats, and sheep.

N.B.—Mange in cattle and scab in sheep are both contagious, but are not of a fatal nature; still, when these diseases are found among stock, the affected animals should be separated from the healthy and placed under medical treatment, to prevent the spread of the diseases and to cure the diseased animals, as mangy cattle and scabby sheep will neither thrive nor fatten.

CHAPTER II.

SOME COMMON COMPLAINTS.

THERE are some complaints among cattle, goats, and sheep that are common—that is to say, in a large herd some of these complaints will always be present. They are simple ailments that can be easily cured, but, even in these simple diseases, great care and proper treatment are absolutely necessary. The least delay or neglect may result in something serious.

I will mention these complaints just as they come to my mind.

1. COUGH.—Sometimes cattle, goats, and sheep are troubled with a dry, hacking cough. Give a lot of bamboo leaves every day, and Aconite Nap. 1x. ten drops every morning, and Nux Vom. 1x. ten drops every evening, until the animal is relieved. Half the quantity for small calves, goats, and sheep. Sometimes from ten drops to half a dram of turpentine in some warm water or castor oil will prove very beneficial. Give the animal a lot of fresh tender bamboo leaves night and morning

for a week, and give half an ounce of condition powder twice a day.

2. WEAK EYES, or watering eyes.—The eye must be well washed with one part of alum and ten parts of cold water three or four times a day.

3. INFLAMMATION OF THE EYES, OR OPHTHALMIA.

Causes.—Blow from a stick or whip; dirt; insect or something in the eye; cold, damp, or excessive heat.

Symptoms.—The eyelids are swollen; tears flow in abundance; there is great sensitiveness to light; the eye is bloodshot and covered with scum.

Treatment.—Examine the eyes and remove all dirt and foreign bodies. Wash with a lotion of ten parts of cold water to one part of alum four times a day.

Give Aconite Nap. lx. and Belladonna lx. alternately, ten drops every four hours, or Euphrasia lx. Half the quantity for small calves, goats, and sheep.

Keep the eye bandaged, and keep the animal out of the sun and damp. Give nourishing and wholesome food.

4. MANGE is an infectious disease.

Causes.—Parasites in the skin, caused by want of cleanliness.

Treatment.—Give the animal four *chittacks* of salt and four *chittacks* of sulphur every morning for a fortnight, then stop the sulphur and continue the salt in two *chittack* doses every morning. Smaller doses for calves, goats, and sheep.

Make a liniment of the following medicines and rub into the affected parts every morning:—

Cocoanut oil	4 chittacks
Spirits of Turpentine	4 chittacks
Gum Camphor	2 chittacks
Ground Sulphur	4 chittacks
Phenyle	1 chittack

The affected parts must be properly washed with hot water and soap and dried before the liniment is rubbed in.

5. DRINKING HER OWN MILK.—If a cow or goat takes to this habit, or a bull-calf licks its own urine or that of another, cradles should be put on their necks. Cradles are made of pieces of bamboo tied together.

If the animals get a sufficient supply of drinking-water and a proper quantity of salt, they will not take to these injurious tricks.

6. BROKEN HORNS.—The horns of cattle, goats, and sheep are subject to accident.

Causes.—Falls, blows, or struggles with each other in fights. The fracture bleeds most freely and may endanger the animal's life.

Symptoms.—The fractures are of three kinds.

1st. The bone is broken, but the horn is not detached, and there is no open wound.

Treatment.—Support the parts with a splint and bandage to keep them steady and at rest, and wet the bandage with Phenyle and water or Arnica and water. The fracture will soon unite.

2nd. The horn is torn away and the bone is left bare and bleeding.

Treatment.—Bandage the part with soft cloth and keep it wet with Phenyle and water or Arnica and water. The horn will not grow again, but a skin will grow and cover the bone.

3rd. Both the bone and the horn are snapped clean off, and there is a large open bleeding wound. Inflammation of the brain or lockjaw may follow, or gangrene set in.

Treatment.—Immediately cut the broken remains of the horn to the level of the wound and bathe it with *cold* water and alum, or with Tincture of Arnica Montana and water, until the bleeding stops; then apply Iodoform, and bandage up properly and apply Phenyle and water. If the animal has any fever and is in pain, give it Aconite Nap. lx. and Arnica Mon. lx. alternately, ten drops every three hours. Half the quantity for goats and sheep.

Great care and cleanliness are necessary to prevent gangrene.

7. Leech in the Nose.—Leeches often worry cattle, goats, and sheep by entering and fixing themselves in the nostrils while the animals are grazing.

Treatment.—Inject a little salt water into the nostril,

and when the leech moves, draw it out with a pair of forceps or *chimtas.* Apply a little dry salt to the part to stop the bleeding.

8. LOSS OF CUD, or arrest of rumination, is not so much a disease as a symptom of disease.

Treatment.—If there is no costiveness, and if no disease can be discovered, give a dose of one ounce of condition powder every morning, or Nux Vom. lx. ten drops four times a day for a week. Half the quantity for small calves, goats, and sheep.

9. WOUNDS AND BRUISES on cattle, goats, or sheep should never be neglected. They are liable to be troublesome and get infested with maggots.

Treatment.—Wash with Arnica and water, or with Phenyle and water, and put a bandage round, and keep it wet with Arnica or Phenyle and water.

Give the animal ten drops of Arnica lx. every four hours if there be much pain. Half the quantity for calves, goats, and sheep.

10. ENLARGED PAPILLÆ OF THE MOUTH.—All ruminating animals have pointed papillæ like points or thorns on the tongue and in the lining of their cheeks.

Symptoms.—These papillæ grow long and hard, and the cheeks, lip, and tongue of the animal grow tender, so that when the cow attempts to eat she is unable to do so. After a few days the mouth becomes yellow and furred and the breath smells very bad. A milking cow's milk will dry up. If care is not taken the animal will die of starvation.

Treatment.—The mouth, tongue, and cheeks must be well washed three or four times a day with a strong solution of alum and warm water.

This disease is caused by a disordered stomach. Give the creature Nux Vom. lx. ten drops every four hours, or one ounce of the condition powder every morning and evening. Half the quantity for calves, goats, and sheep.

The animal must have plenty of rice or wheat gruel three times a day, with a *chittack* of salt in it each time.

If she will not drink the gruel, give it in a horn or bamboo *chonga.* Cattle that have sufficient salt regularly in their food are seldom troubled with this disease.

11. LAMPAS.—Horses generally get this disease, but in India cattle often suffer from it.

Causes.—Deranged stomach or bowels, or worms.

Symptoms.—The gums of the upper jaw swell, and often are very painful, so much so that the animal cannot eat its food. When you strike the place with your finger, it sounds as if it were inflated. The animal cannot bear to have you press it hard.

Treatment.—Some burn the swelling with a hot iron, but this is a most barbarous and useless practice. The common treatment adopted by natives is to fill the cavity on the front of the upper jaw with a little Asafœtida and cotton.

The proper treatment is to give the animal Nux Vom. lx. ten drops every four hours, or one ounce of the condition powder every morning; and rub the swollen part well with salt. Half quantity for calves, goats, and sheep.

12. WASTING IN CALVES.—Very often calves refuse their food or do not eat well; if neglected, they gradually become emaciated, and some severe illness follows. A calf will never refuse food if it be in good health, unless the food be dirty or otherwise unpleasant.

Loss of appetite is always a symptom of sickness. As soon as you find a calf refuse its food, examine it carefully and see what is wrong. If no disease can be discovered, change its food; if, even then, it will not eat, give it two drams of the condition powder every morning and evening, or Nux Vom. lx. and Arsenicum Alb. lx. alternately, four drops every three hours.

If you find the symptoms continue in spite of the medicine, continue the medicine for a week or ten days.

If the symptoms be caused by worms in the stomach, then adopt the treatment prescribed for worms.

13. HIDE-BOUND.—This is not a disease but a symptom of disease.

Causes.—Disordered stomach, poor and insufficient food, exposure to cold and damp weather.

Symptoms.—The hair looks rough and clotted, the

natural smoothness and gloss being absent; the skin feels hard, tough, and fixed to the flesh. The animal becomes dull and listless, does not eat well, and loses flesh.

The hair begins to fall off. The creature gets weaker every day, until it sits or falls down and cannot rise again. Sometimes it begins to purge, and a discharge comes from the mouth, and the creature dies. I have seen many calves suffer in this way.

Treatment.—The cause of the hide-bound must be found out, and the disease of which it is a symptom must be treated accordingly.

If no special disease be discoverable, then give Nux Vom. Ix. and Arsenicum Alb. Ix. alternately, from five to ten drops every four hours, until improvement, or give two drams of the condition powder every morning and evening.

Accessory Treatment.—Rice or wheat gruel must be given to the animal. Give salt in its food. Wherever the cattle are properly fed and cared for, hide-bound is never seen. Pure drinking-water must be given in abundance.

Also, mix three *chittacks* of Mustard oil, one *chittack* of Sulphur, one *chittack* of Camphor, one *chittack* of Spirits of Turpentine, and quarter of a *chittack* of Phenyle, and rub the animal all over the body twice a week. If no disease prevails, and the animal is not too weak, bathe it in warm water and with soap before applying the ointment. But be careful to thoroughly dry the animal after its bath.

14. COLD OR CATARRH.—Calves and milk-cows, sheep and goats, are often afflicted with this disease.

Causes.—The disease is caused by exposure to draughts or wet, over-crowding in the house, dirty, damp house, or not drying after bathing.

Symptoms.—The nose is dry, the eyes are watery, there is a discharge from the nostrils, the animal stands in one place as if stiff in the limbs, and does not chew her cud properly. There is more or less fever, and sometimes cough and purging.

Treatment.—It requires to be immediately attended to, or it will end in some very dangerous illness. It is very frequent and fatal in calves. Give Aconite Nap. 1x. and Arsenicum Alb. 1x. alternately, five drops every two hours, or Fowler's Solution of Arsenic, ten drops in a little water three times a day.

Should the discharge become thick, and the nostrils and the eyes swollen, give Aconite 1x. and Mercurius Sol. 1x. alternately, every two hours.

Accessory Treatment.—Separate the animal from the rest, and keep it warm and quiet. Cover it with a blanket, and keep it in a warm but well-ventilated place.

No liquid must be given to the creature for twenty-four hours. Bo one or two *seers* of ground wheat, and give in a thick mash. When the animal begins to improve, after twenty-four hours give it warm wheat or barley gruel to drink.

I have found the homœopathic treatment very successful.

15. SPRAINS. — The muscles, or ligaments of the joints of the legs or tendons, become ruptured or sprained. The part swells and becomes hot and very painful, and the animal is quite lame.

Treatment.—As soon as detected, the injured parts should be bound up with a splint and bandage, and kept at rest, the bandage being kept wet with a lotion of cold water and Tincture of Arnica or Aconite. When the swelling and pain lessen, rub the part well with the hand.

16. DISLOCATION sometimes results from accident or over-exertion, a bone being put out of joint. It is a very painful thing, and may terminate seriously if neglected for even a short time. A surgeon should be called in at once.

Treatment. — If no surgeon be available, throw the animal down gently, so as to have the dislocated joint uppermost, and then seize the leg and pull it downwards.

The bone will be heard to return to its socket with a snap. After which, rest and cold water and Arnica application is all that is necessary. If there be much pain and swelling, a little Tincture of Aconite instead of Arnica may be applied to the part; or the Belladonna liniment applied twice a day.

17. SORE FEET.

Causes.—Foreign bodies, such as gravel, dirt, thorns, etc., in the cleft of the foot. If cattle are kept in wet and dirty places they will be troubled with sore feet.

Symptoms.—Lameness, swelling of the pasterns, pain. Matter forms, and unless let out and properly treated, ulcers form and become very troublesome and injurious.

Treatment.—Examine the feet carefully, and remove all dirt and foreign matters that may be found. Remove all dead hoof and pare the hoof properly. Wash the feet with warm water and poultice with linseed meal or bran. Let out the matter if there be any. Wash the feet with Phenyle and water, and bandage up the sore foot, and keep applying Phenyle and water. The part must be kept perfectly clean. Ten drops of Silicea 6x. should be given internally, morning and night.

18. COSTIVENESS in cattle may terminate very seriously, if neglected.

Cause.—Dry, hard, and unwholesome food.

Treatment.—Give from one to two *chittacks* of Eno's Fruit Salt in a quart of warm water; or quarter of a *seer* of Epsom salt in a *seer* of warm water; quarter of an hour after, give two quarts of thin, warm rice gruel.

Let it have no food until it is purged, and then give it Nux Vom. Ix. ten drops every three hours during that day, and soft food in small quantities; or give one ounce of condition powder every morning for a week, and feed on bran mash.

19. Irregular Teeth.

Symptoms.—The beast eats less food than usual, and becomes gradually thinner and weaker; half-chewed food and saliva dribble from the mouth; the animal is hoven at times, and a bad smell issues from the mouth; the sides of the cheek are ulcerated, caused by the irregular teeth.

Treatment.—The mouth must be carefully examined, and all long or irregular teeth must be shortened and smoothed by means of a tooth-rasp. If there be a decayed tooth or an abscess under the tooth, the tooth must be drawn out.

20. The Navel ill.—Occasionally calves, kids, and lambs suffer from this disease.

Caused by the abrupt or imperfect separation of the navel cord, which makes the navel bleed; want of cleanliness and proper care.

Treatment.—If the cord be of sufficient length, a ligature might be passed around the end and tied, but if close to the abdomen, a little burnt alum with a piece of lint tied on to the part will suffice to stop the bleeding, and the wound will soon heal.

If not attended to at once, an abscess may form in the part, and may lead to internal inflammation and cause death, or flies may blow the sore and breed maggots.

If an abscess form, follow the treatment prescribed for abscess. If maggots form, use the maggot destroyer.

21. Sore Teats.

Causes.—The calf nipping the nipples; leaving the nipples wet after milking; cold; strong winds; want of cleanliness.

Symptoms.—The nipples get chapped and inflamed; sometimes little pimples and sores form on the nipples; the cow becomes troublesome at milking, and kicks about; she refuses to allow the calf to suck; the teats become very painful, and give forth a discharge which mingles with the milk; the milk lessens; inflammation of the udder may set in.

Treatment.—Wash the teats well with warm water, dry perfectly, and apply some Hydrastis Can. ointment, or Camphor ointment, morning and evening. Great care must be taken to gently draw out every drop of milk; if necessary, the teat-tube must be used. Any rough treatment may make the cow vicious and spoil her.

Preventive.—Keep the teats clean and dry; rub some butter or mustard oil on them every time the cow is milked.

CHAPTER III.

DANGEROUS BUT NOT CONTAGIOUS DISEASES.

1. CALVING.—Some cows have great trouble at the time of calving, and need proper medical treatment. If it be a cross-birth, or if the trouble be caused by contraction or deformity in the bone of the pelvis, or from tumours, dropsy, or the large size of the calf, the management will require professional knowledge and skill. Simple causes of the difficulty may be successfully treated thus:—

Protracted labour.—If labour pains continue long, give Gelseminum lx. ten drops every half-hour or twenty minutes.

After-pains.—After labour, if there be any pains, or to prevent any after-pains, give Mother Tincture of Arnica Mon. ten drops every hour or two. Give four doses only.

The after-birth or placenta, unless discharged soon after calving, may cause fever and general derangement. Give Pulsatilla lx. ten drops three times a day. If this fails to effect the desired end in twelve hours, then give Secale lx. in the same way.

Flooding.—Allow the cow to lie down, and keep her quiet, with the hinder parts rather higher than the lower. A bandage must be applied tightly round the belly, and a cloth wet in cold water must be applied to the vagina and over the loins. Injections of cold water must be thrown up the fundament every half-hour.

The best medicines for flooding are Sabina and Secale: China is also very useful.

When the blood is black and smells bad, give Secale Cer. (Ergot of rye) 1x. ten drops every fifteen or thirty minutes until flooding stops.

When the blood is bright red, give Sabina (Savine) 1x. ten drops every fifteen or thirty minutes.

Accessory Treatment.—Great care must be taken to give the cow quiet and rest.

Do nothing that will excite her. Do not force her to lie down. Do not force the medicine down her throat. Give the medicine in a piece of bread or in her drinking-water.

2. SLIPPING DOWN OF THE WOMB is a common complaint with large, loose-limbed cows, especially if they are old, and have had many calves. This is a complaint that the people of India do not know how to treat, and they generally let the poor animal suffer and die: and if a cow is known to be liable to this trouble, they will not buy her at any price, however low.

Cause.—The convulsive efforts made to expel the fœtus.

Symptoms.—The womb is thrown out, and hangs between the hind-legs of the animal.

Treatment.—This complaint only wants care. Immediately the womb slips it should be carefully washed with lukewarm water and alum, and then replaced, and an alum and cold water injection given. No force should be used in attempts to replace the womb, but it should be gently and carefully pushed up by a process of kneading till the whole is up into the pelvic cavity, and then it should be retained by the hand for a time, till the spasms begin to subside, when the hand may be gently drawn away. The vagina should be supported by a bandage of strong cloth six inches broad.

The cow must not be allowed to sit down, and she must be watched and not allowed to strain when in pain; if she does, or if her eyes appear glassy, she should receive proper medicines.

If not replaced at once, the womb may mortify and fall out.

If the services of an experienced doctor can be obtained, he should be immediately called.

Give the animal Mother Tincture of Arnica Mon. ten drops every hour, or Mother Tincture of Belladonna five drops every hour, for a day or two.

The alum lotion used for injection must be made by dissolving one part of alum in eight or ten parts of *cold* water.

Accessory Treatment.—The cow must be kept perfectly quiet and confined to her stall, and have some warm rice or wheat gruel given her three times a day. No heating food should be given to the cow for a week or ten days.

3. Swollen Udder in milk-cows is a very serious symptom, and if not taken in hand at once may lead to much distress, and dry up the cow and prevent her from ever milking again.

Causes.—It is a tendency to gathering caused by a chill or a bruise, or some injury to the udder before or after calving, or by too high feeding before calving. If the cow is bathed, or her udder washed and not dried properly, her udder may swell. If there is a great secretion of milk before calving, and the milk is not extracted, it is likely to coagulate and cause inflammation. If the cow is not properly milked, and some milk is left in the udder, it may cause inflammation. Sometimes, giving the cow *cold* water to drink after she has calved causes it.

Symptoms.—One of the first signs of inflammation is, the cow objecting to the bumping of the calf's nose. The udder is somewhat swollen and painful; there is some difficulty in extracting the milk. Then little hard lumps can be felt in the teats or in some part of the bag. The pulse is full, quick, and hard; the breathing quick and hard. The breathing quickens, the mouth and horns become hot, bowels are bound, and other symptoms of fever are present. If the disease is allowed to go on, the fever will become more severe; the cow will not eat or chew her cud; the hard swelling will become soft in consequence of matter having formed; the milk will become mixed with matter and blood.

If the matter is not let out, it will spread through the udder, at the same time making its way slowly to the skin, through which it at last bursts, leaving deep long ulcers. These heal with great difficulty, and in many cases a portion of the udder or the whole is lost. If this result is avoided by judicious treatment, some hardening of the bag may, nevertheless, remain, which will take some time to remove.

Treatment.—The ordinary treatment is as follows:—As soon as it is observed that the udder is swollen or painful and there is difficulty in extracting the milk, *neem* leaves should be boiled, and the pot put under the udder, so that the steam may pass over the affected parts. The affected parts should be thoroughly fomented with the boiled *neem* leaves, after which the udder should be properly wiped and gently rubbed with the Belladonna liniment, and the calf allowed to suck in order to draw off some of the inflammation. There is danger of the calf becoming ill by drinking the milk of an inflamed udder, so it is best to get the milk out of the udder by milking or by means of the teat-tube or a pump. Give the cow two or three *chittacks* of Eno's Fruit Salt and a quarter of a *seer* of common salt in warm water, or half a *seer* of Epsom salt, and keep her in a warm place. This treatment should be repeated two or three times a day until the bowels are freely moved.

Native Treatment.—At the very commencement of the trouble, make a paste of pounded *huldee* (turmeric) and lime (such as is eaten in *pan*), mix and well smear the whole udder, and give the animal from a pint to a quart of castor oil in warm water. Foment frequently with *neem* leaves.

Homœopathic Treatment.—As soon as the least symptom of inflammation is detected, give internally Aconitum Nap. 1x. and Bry. Alb. 1x. ten drops, alternately every three hours; foment the affected part with boiled *neem* leaves, and gently rub the part with the Belladonna liniment.

If the inflammation increases, give, internally, Belladonna 1x. ten drops every three hours. If no improvement takes place, in order to expedite the formation of matter give Hepar Sulp. 3x. one grain every four hours, and bring the gathering to a head by putting on a linseed poultice.

If the gathering softens, the matter must be let out with a lancet, and a poultice kept to the wound until it begins to heal up. The poultice must be renewed night and morning. If the wound looks or smells in the least offensive, wash it out thoroughly with Hydrastis and water or Phenyle and water.

Accessory Treatment.—The cow must be put on simple food, as rice gruel and *doob* grass. Put salt in the food. The drinking-water must *not* be cold, but lukewarm. Rest and quiet are very necessary.

Preventive.—If the udder fills with milk many days before the calf is born, extract the milk and empty the udder every morning and evening until the calf is born, and rub the whole udder with warm Mustard oil with a little Camphor in it. Immediately after the birth of the calf draw out every drop of milk and rub the udder with Mustard oil and Camphor. Also avoid the causes of the complaint.

4. RHEUMATISM.—This disease is rather common in some districts in India.

Causes.—Exposure to wet and damp, and draughts; damp floors; bad food; bad water.

Symptoms.—The animal becomes dull and droops, and is disinclined to move. There is loss of appetite; pain in the back; one or more of the joints become inflamed and painful; the animal moves with difficulty. Sometimes there is much fever. The complaint may last for only a few days, but is liable to return with change of weather.

Treatment.—Give Aconite Nap. lx. and Rhus Tox. lx. alternately, ten drops every two hours. Bry. Alb. also is a very good remedy for rheumatism; it should be given after Aconite. Apply Rhus Tox. ointment to the affected parts. The parts must be fomented three or four times a day with boiled *neem* leaves.

Accessory Treatment.—Place the animal in a warm and dry south room, and cover it with a blanket, and bandage the affected part with flannel. The creature should be fed on boiled wheat or gram, and *doob* grass.

5. PARALYSIS.—Total or partial loss of sensibility and motion in one or more parts of the animal.

Causes.—Injuries to the spine from blows; or in pack-bullocks, from over-loading; sudden changes of temperature and exposure to wet and cold or excessive heat. Some kinds of grain and herbs will cause it.

Symptoms.—The animal staggers and drops its hind-legs; loss of power in the limbs, and inability to move freely. It falls and is unable to rise again; pulse full and slow, and loss of appetite; the bowels are bound, and the urine is retained, or the urine and dung are passed involuntarily.

Treatment.—Give Belladonna lx. and Nux Vom. lx. alternately, ten drops every three hours. Rub the back and limbs with boiled *neem* leaves and salt.

Accessory Treatment.—Place the animal in a dry and

warm room, with lots of straw to lie upon. Turn her over twice a day, and give her a change of food. Great care and patience are needed.

6. HOVEN.—Distension of the first stomach or rumen with gas or wind. It is a common disease among cattle.

Causes.—Irregular feeding; eating food that the animal has not been accustomed to. Animals that have been almost starved for some time, when put into rich pasture or given grain, over-feed themselves, and the undissolved food undergoes chemical changes, and gas or wind is given off. Pasturing on marshy or inundated places, or eating fermented grass or food.

Symptoms.—The symptoms appear suddenly and run their course rapidly. Swelling in the back portion of the left side of the belly, which, on being tapped with the fingers, is found to consist of wind in the first stomach; breathing is difficult; the animal neither eats nor chews the cud; the head is poked out; the animal grunts, stands quite stiffly, and appears unable to move; the eyes become red and thrust out of their sockets; the mouth is filled with frothy saliva, and the tongue hangs out of the mouth; the back is crouched, the legs drawn under the body; should the animal lie down, the breathing becomes more difficult; the animal falls and struggles violently; sometimes sour fluid and food are discharged from the mouth and nostrils; lastly, death ensues.

This disease is very often mistaken for other diseases, and is sometimes thought to be the effect of poison, on account of the very rapid way it runs its course. In acute cases the duration of the disease may be from one to three hours; in more protracted cases, the symptoms may continue for twelve hours.

Treatment.—Give the animal forty drops of Rubini's Tincture of Camphor, in a wineglassful of water, two doses at an interval of ten or fifteen minutes. After fifteen minutes from the time you have given the second dose, give Nux Vom. 1x. and Bry. Alb. 1x. alternately, ten drops in water every hour or half-hour. An enema of two *seers* of warm water of 103° temperature with four ounces of Glycerine dissolved in it will relieve the animal. Wash the mouth with clean water. If the case is severe, and after giving the above medicines no improvement takes place in a little while, the trocar must be used. The trocar must be plunged inward and downward into the paunch, through the left side of the stomach, midway between the last rib and the haunch-bone.

Accessory Treatment.—Give the animal thin rice gruel and soft green grass in small quantities, and plenty of salt for a few days after improvement sets in. Also give half an ounce of condition powder every day.

7. Grain-sick.—Impaction of the rumen or first stomach with food, either of a coarse or tough and

indigestible kind, such as over-ripe *wooloo*-grass, reeds, or uncooked whole grain.

Causes.—Indigestible and coarse grass or reeds; unground and uncooked grain; too large a quantity of food; insufficient supply of drinking-water. When the stomach is over-loaded it becomes at first torpid in action, and from the continued pressure and distension of its muscular coats it ceases to act on account of the latter becoming powerless.

Symptoms.—The symptoms are somewhat like those in hoven. In hoven the stomach is filled with gas; the left flank, on pressure, feels soft, elastic, and yielding to the fingers; on percussion, it sounds hollow and drum-like; frequent belching; the wind that escapes has an offensive smell; respiration quick, short, and puffing; position standing, head stretched forward, unable to move; moans, and appears in great distress; eyes red and staring. In grain-sick the stomach is packed with food. The symptoms appear gradually. The animal is dull and does not chew the cud; the left flank gradually swells, and when tapped with the finger or pressed on, is hard and pits as if pressing upon soft earth. The bowels are inclined to be constipated; the animal generally keeps standing; fluid and food are discharged from the mouth and nose; the animal grinds its teeth and grunts. As the contents of the stomach ferment, the stomach becomes more distended; the pulse becomes weak and small, the respiration becomes more difficult. Death is caused from suffocation. The disease lasts from one to three days.

Treatment.—Give the animal Nux Vom. 1x. ten drops every hour; allow it to drink as much water as it will drink. If the animal seems to be in much pain, then before giving it Nux Vom. give it forty drops of Rubini's Camphor in a little warm water, two doses at an interval of fifteen minutes. An enema of two *seers* of hot water and four ounces of Glycerine should be given if the bowels continue very much bound. If inflammation of the stomach follows, give Belladonna 1x. ten drops every hour. Inflammation is recognised by pressure on the distended stomach giving the animal pain.

When the medicines fail to act, and the symptoms increase in severity, the stomach must be relieved by cutting it open and taking out the contents. Plunge a sharp penknife into the flanks between the last rib and the point of the hip-bone; cut from above about two inches from the cross-bones of the loins downwards; make an incision about six inches long through the walls of the belly, and then cut through the walls of the stomach, and remove with the hand all the food.

When all the food is removed, pour into the stomach two or three *chittacks* of Eno's Fruit Salt and a *seer* of warm water. Then sew up the hole in the stomach and afterwards the opening in the flanks. But before doing so, first well wash the wounds with Phenyle and water (one to ten parts) and afterwards dress the wound with Iodoform. Great care must be taken that gangrene does not set in. The wound must be washed and redressed twice a day. This operation requires a practised hand.

Accessory Treatment.—The animal must have nothing but rice and wheat gruel for two or three days. After which small quantities of fresh young *doob* grass should be given in addition to the gruel. Give the animal plenty of salt, and pure drinking-water. Also give one ounce of the condition powder every day for a week.

Preventive.—Give the animal soft food in moderate quantities; give abundance of pure drinking-water at least three times a day. Hard and dry substances should not be allowed. Food should not be given in very large quantities or too frequently.

8. FARDEL-BOUND.—Impaction of the third stomach with hard, dry, and indigestible food, which accumulates and becomes so very hard, dry, and caked between the folds or leaves of the stomach as to always arrest more or less its functions, and in severe cases to cause total obstruction.

Causes.—This disease occurs more frequently in the hot season, and is common in a season when there is an unusual scarcity of pasture and water. Cattle and sheep are then driven from sheer hunger to eat hard and fibrous grasses and reeds, or branches of shrubs, and trees, and the third stomach is unable to grind down such hard and unwholesome fodder, and the latter gradually accumulates, hardens, and cakes within the stomach.

Symptoms.—The animal does not chew the cud; there is a loss of appetite; respiration is quickened, and is accompanied by a grunt, not unlike the grunt which is heard in pleuro-pneumonia. The bowels are constipated sometimes at the commencement; there is slight diarrhœa, but, as a rule, there is constipation; now and then a small amount of liquid fæces, with very hard and dark-coloured pieces of the caked fodder, detached from the leaves of the third stomach, is passed; the urine is high coloured, and not unfrequently there are signs of hoven.

If relief is not afforded, inflammation of the stomach sets in. In this case the respiration becomes increased, and the grunting more audible. The animal grinds its teeth, and its countenance is peculiarly expressive of pain: the mouth, ears, and horns become cold, the pulse very small and thready, and numbers from eighty-five to a hundred. Any dung passed is partly liquid and partly in small hard cakes, and very offensive. The grunt now becomes a moan. Sometimes, in the last stage the animal will be in a state of stupor; in some cases symptoms of great excitement occur, and these probably depend upon the fourth stomach having become inflamed. The duration of the disease is from five to fifteen days.

Treatment.—The treatment must be with the view of relieving the over-loaded and impacted stomach of its hard, dry, and caked contents.

Give the animal Eno's Fruit Salt, from two to four *chittacks* in a *seer* of hot water, two doses at an interval of fifteen minutes. Foment the stomach. Half an hour after you have given the salt, give Nux Vom. lx. and Belladonna lx. alternately, ten drops every hour or two.

Accessory Treatment.—Give the creature plenty of thin warm gruel (rice or wheat) at short intervals during the day and night.

This will assist much in opening the bowels, and in softening the caked food in the third stomach and facilitating its escape. Very often many days elapse before all the hard stuff is got rid of; therefore it is necessary to continue giving the gruel until no hard caked pieces are found in the dung. After the animal has recovered, give it soft green grass in small quantities.

Preventive.—Soft and easily digestible food, abundance of drinking-water, and regular supply of salt.

9. CHOKING.—Difficulty in swallowing or inability to swallow.

Cause.—This condition may be caused by hard and large pieces of food, such as sugar-cane, *kirby*, etc., becoming lodged in the back part of the throat or in any part of the gullet—the channel by which the food passes from the mouth to the stomach.

Sometimes foreign bodies, such as pieces of leather, iron, nails, sharp thorns, sharp pieces of wood, etc., are taken by cattle and become lodged in the gullet, and when very hard, with sharp edges or points, may lacerate the lining membrane of the tube.

Symptoms.—If the obstruction is in the back part of the mouth or throat, the animal coughs and salivates, and when drinking, the water will be returned by the nostrils.

If in the gullet, after making two or three swallows, and filling the gullet as far as the point of obstruction, the water will be returned by the mouth and nostrils.

The animal is very uneasy; his countenance shows signs of pain; spasmodic or cramp-like actions of the muscles of the neck will be observed. These are owing to the animal endeavouring to make the lodged body go down into the stomach, or to be returned by the mouth. In a little time signs of hoven appear, and if the animal be not soon relieved, the left side of the belly will become much swollen.

If the obstruction is in the throat, by introducing the hand into the very back part of the mouth it will be felt.

If it is in that part of the gullet between the back part of the mouth and the chest, it will be felt on the outside by carefully examining the throat with the hand, as there will be a swelling at the point of obstruction.

If it is lodged in that part of the gullet which passes through the chest, then the negative evidence of its not being found in the back part of the mouth, or any part of the throat, will be conclusive; and when the animal drinks, water will be observed passing down the gullet along the lower part of the throat without meeting with any impediment; but after the animal has taken two or three swallows, the gullet, at the throat portion, will gradually become filled with the water, until at last, when quite filled up to its junction with the throat, vomition of it will occur.

Treatment.—Give very carefully and gradually warm linseed oil, half a pint, with *arrack* two ounces, well mixed together.

This will lubricate the gullet and the impacted food or foreign body, and stimulate the gullet to act, and force it onward.

The medicine may be returned by vomition once or oftener, but it must be perseveringly given again and again, and only a little at a time.

If the cause of obstruction is lodged in the back part of the throat, it must be removed by the hand; if in the throat portion of the gullet, after giving the oil and *arrack* press with the fingers all round the swelling observed in the throat, and it will very often be thus removed a little, then give a little more of the oil and *arrack* and again apply more pressure to the swelling; and by so persevering the impacted body will generally pass onwards, and the animal will be relieved.

If by the symptoms it is evident that the part of the gullet within the chest is obstructed, and the steady perseverance in giving the oil and *arrack* has failed to remove it, then a hollow elastic tube, if at hand, may be introduced by the mouth down the gullet to the part obstructed, and a little gentle pressure will generally move the cause of obstruction onwards to the stomach. If a proper tube is not to be obtained, then a good rattan cane, about the thickness of the forefinger, with a soft ball of cotton or tow about the size of an egg, covered with cloth, and securely fastened around the one end of the cane, may, after being well soaked in oil, be introduced by the mouth into the gullet, and pressed gently against the impacted body. During this operation the mouth must be kept open by an assistant.

It now and then happens that the gullet is cut or torn by the impacted body, or by the operator using too much force with the tube, or from the ball not being properly fastened on the end of the rattan cane, and thus the gullet may become permanently injured, and in such a case choking is very apt to recur.

Whenever choking happens, the part of the gullet obstructed will remain weak for some days, so only soft food, such as gruel or mashes, must be given for three or four days, and afterwards young green grass.

Opening the throat portion of the gullet with a knife, when the obstruction is in that part, is, in extreme cases, practised by veterinary surgeons.

10. RED-WATER.—This is a blood disease, resulting from imperfect digestion of the food and the consequent faulty preparation of the blood, etc., and the blood becomes thin and weak.

It is accompanied with much prostration and debility, and in severe cases with emaciation. Both cattle and sheep are liable to the disease; more frequently cows and ewes are attacked, especially a short time after parturition and probably this depends upon the drain on the system by the secretion of milk.

Causes.—Some undrained lands are known to yield pasture which causes this disease. The pasture may be very rank, non-nutritious, or bare, and mixed with acrid herbage. It has been proved that when such lands are properly drained, manured, and cultivated, cattle pasturing on them cease to suffer from red-water.

The disease very often attacks the cattle of poor people, who cannot feed them properly. Foul water off boggy lands will produce the disease. It occurs more frequently at those seasons when the animals change their coats.

Cattle fed on poor lands, especially when badly drained and not manured, are very subject to the disease; indeed, it may be ascribed to unwholesome food and water, and particularly to food which, though bulky, contains a small amount of nutriment (such as paddy-straw), and consequently the blood becomes poor and thin in quality, and doubtless contains noxious matters, which nature attempts to remove by the urine.

Symptoms.—At first an animal shows signs of not thriving well, and, now and then, of being ill, by not feeding well and not regularly chewing the cud; and if a milk-cow, by giving less milk. The coat stares, and the skin is dry, unhealthy, and very often has a yellowish tinge; the back is arched; the animal is found alone, away from the rest of the stock: diarrhœa sets in, and may continue for two or three days, and then the bowels become costive.

The flanks are hollow, sometimes signs of hoven appear, or symptoms of abdominal pain may be present. The urine, up to this time, is found slightly altered, being perhaps only a little tinged. As long as the diarrhœa continues, the urine remains but little affected: but when constipation sets in, it at once becomes altered in colour, being at first red, or of a claret colour, and the animal evinces pain in passing it. Constipation generally sets in about the fourth day, and then the urine is more frequently passed, and becomes very dark, and sometimes so dark as to cause the name of black-water to be given to the disease.

The urine is also offensive in odour.

The animal becomes very weak; the lining membranes of the mouth and eyelids are pale in colour; the eyes are sunk; the mouth, ears, and legs cold; the pulse very weak; respiration rapid; the animal lies down much, loses condition rapidly, and soon becomes emaciated. Signs of abdominal pain are frequent; the animal becomes very weak, and is unable to rise; death ensues.

The duration of the disease is from five to twenty-five days.

Treatment.—Give Aconite Nap. lx. and Bry. Alb. lx., or Nux Vom. lx. alternately, ten drops every two hours.

Accessory Treatment.—Abundance of good wheat gruel must be given frequently, and the animal kept in a dry and warm place.

Preventive.—Good pasturage, regular supply of salt and drinking-water, and proper shelter.

11. Indigestion and Diarrhœa.—This disease consists in frequent purging, generally without fever or con-

stitutional disturbance; but sometimes with signs of abdominal irritation. The frequent and inordinate passing of watery fæces results from a disordered state of the stomach and bowels.

Causes.—It generally arises from the animal having taken some unwholesome forage, acrid herbage, or foul water. Indigestion is frequently the cause of diarrhœa.

The herbage grown on certain lands produces it, and very often such lands are marshy and badly drained. In the Panjáb it is known by the name of *chooknee*, and has of late years attacked the cattle of that province in seasons when pasturage and water were scarce, and the animals were obliged to eat unwholesome herbage and acrid shrubs, and drink very foul water.

An over-dose of purgative medicine may also cause diarrhœa. Again, in cases where the stomach and bowels become over-loaded, diarrhœa may follow.

In the last stages of pleuro-pneumonia and other blood diseases, looseness of the bowels invariably appears. Cold or sudden chill has been known to produce it, specially when the bowels have been in an unhealthy condition.

Exposure to great heat is sometimes another cause.

Diarrhœa generally attacks herds when grazing on lands yielding the first shoots of green grass after the first fall of the rains.

Symptoms.—A frequent passing of watery dung with wind; at first with no straining or pain.

The appetite generally remains good; the rumination may be a little irregular, and the secretion of milk may be less than usual; but the general health of the animal seems but little affected.

If the purging continue long, then there will be straining at the time of passing fæces, and the back will be arched; more or less pain will be shown, and sometimes blood will be passed with the dung.

This disease in the Panjáb is generally fatal, because the original cause of the disease remains in operation.

Treatment.—Give the animal Arsenicum Alb. lx. ten drops every two hours. If there be any pain or blood in the motions, give Mer. Cor. lx. five drops every two hours. Half the quantity for calves, sheep, and goats. Do not check the diarrhœa at once; if it continues more than four or five hours, then give medicine.

Half to one ounce of the condition powder given twice a day with some bail fruit dissolved in half a *seer* of water will cure diarrhœa.

Accessory Treatment.—Clean water, soft, sweet, and wholesome grass, and wheat or gram gruel. After the diarrhœa has stopped, give the animal five drops of Nux Vom. lx. twice a day, or half a dram of the condition powder twice a day.

12. Epilepsy.

Causes.—Young, well-fed, fat cattle are the most liable to it. Exposure to the sun in the hot weather and over-exertion on a hot day will cause it.

Symptoms.—The beast staggers and falls suddenly; often bellows in the most alarming manner; every part of the body is violently convulsed; the tail is lashed, the teeth are ground, the mouth closed, and the jaws fastened together; the breathing is quick, and attended with heaving at the flanks; frothy saliva dribbles from the mouth, and the power to retain urine and dung is lost. The convulsions become gradually less severe, then they cease, and the animal seems as if nothing had happened out of the usual way.

Treatment.—During the fit make the animal inhale some musk, and bathe the face and head with cold water. Nothing more can be done during the fit, but as one attack is apt to be followed by others, the treatment must aim at their prevention and cure. Give the animal Belladonna 1x. and Nux Vom. 1x. alternately, ten drops morning and evening. Fits are apt to recur at regular intervals or periodically. A little while before such times the medicines should be given at intervals of one hour.

13. Apoplexy.

Causes.—Sudden rush of blood to the head, followed

by effusion of blood on the brain producing pressure and terminating in some lesion of the blood-vessels, caused by excessive heat and over-exertion or over-feeding.

Symptoms.—Sudden insensibility with loss of sensation and motion. The attack is sudden, but the premonitory symptoms are, general listlessness, and indisposition to motion; breathing low and somewhat laboured; slight fulness and protrusion of the eyeballs. When the animal is struck down, the breathing becomes stertorous, slow, and laboured; the pulse is full and slow; frothy mucus issues from the mouth; the skin becomes cold, eyes glassy, bowels torpid; struggles violently for a time, and dies.

The animal may linger for from one to twenty-four hours.

Treatment.—Pour cold water from a height on the head and back for some time, and give the following remedies.

If from heat, give Belladonna 1x. and Aconite Nap. 1x. alternately, ten drops every half-hour until consciousness returns; then every two hours.

If from over-feeding, give Belladonna 1x. and Nux Vom. 1x. alternately, ten drops in the same way as the above.

Give an enema of two *seers* of hot water and four ounces of Glycerine.

Accessory Treatment.—The animal will remain weak for some time, and must be fed only on gruel and a little soft grass. Quiet and rest are very necessary.

15

An animal once attacked will always be very susceptible to the sun and heat.

14. Inflammation of the Brain.

Causes.—Fracture of the horn; blow on the skull; hydatids in the brain.

Symptoms.—Dulness and heaviness; eyes staring and congested; hurried respiration; full and slow pulse; delirium; the animal rushes at everyone before it, and gallops about with raised tail and arched neck; tears up the soil with its horns and feet; bellows; at last it tumbles down quite exhausted.

Treatment.—It is often best to put a bullet through the head of the beast. A cow, buffalo, or horse cannot be approached or secured while in this state without very great risk.

But if the animal can be secured, give it the following remedies:—Aconite Nap. lx. and Belladonna lx. alternately, ten drops every two hours. Arnica Mon. lx. and Gelseminum lx. will also be helpful. Give the animal four ounces of Eno's Fruit Salt in one *seer* of warm water.

Not many animals recover from this disease.

Accessory Treatment.—Nothing but thin gruel should be given to the animal until the symptoms abate.

15. Colic or Gripes.

Causes.—Cold; chill; rotten food: uncooked grain:

tough grass; fowls' or other birds' droppings; bad water.

Symptoms.—Pain in the stomach, indicated by uneasiness and restlessness; pawing the ground; striking the stomach with the hind-legs or horns; frequent getting up and lying down; grinding the teeth, moaning, etc. If it arises from the presence of wind in the stomach, a swelling will be observed in the stomach on the left side: the wind will pass from the fundament and the mouth.

Treatment.—Give Rubini's Camphor, forty drops every fifteen or twenty minutes, four times, after which give Belladonna 1x. and Nux Vom. 1x. alternately, ten drops every half-hour for a couple of hours, and then every two hours. When the attack is brought on by drinking impure water, give Bry. Alb. 1x. instead of Belladonna.

If the above remedies are not at hand, then give the following mixture. Brandy, four *chittacks*; block salt, half a *chittack*; powdered ginger, half a *chittack*; Bishop's seed (ujwain), two *tolas*; Opium, twenty grains; Camphor (gum), twenty grains. Mix well and give in one dose. From a quarter to half the quantity for calves, goats, and sheep. Ten minutes after this medicine has been given, give the animal a quart of hot water to drink. I got this prescription from a friend who has used it very successfully, but I prefer the first-named remedies.

Cows seldom get colic, but half-grown bulls often do.

Accessory Treatment.—A man should be set to rub on

each side, over the place where the pain is, unless the cow is large with calf, when rubbing must not be resorted to.

Give the animal only warm gruel, and no other food for a day or two. Plenty of salt is necessary in the food.

Preventive.—Avoid the causes.

16. WARBLES.—This name designates a disease which occurs especially in warm weather, and is caused by the gadfly piercing the skin upon the cow's back for the purpose of depositing one or more of its eggs. The result of this is a small swelling, which the insect of the hatched egg occupies until the following hot weather or rains, when it makes its escape, and in a short time becomes a fly on its own account, propagating the species by the same process that begot itself. There may, of course, be numerous swellings upon the cow's back, and each is the temporary habitation of the grub of the gadfly.

They sometimes very seriously injure the general health and condition of the animal, and invariably injure the hide by riddling it with holes, and cause the animal great irritation.

The following is an extract from an English paper:—

"The bot-fly, or warble-fly, is a very widespread pest, and inflicts great suffering and injury on the animals affected by it. The parent-insect lays its eggs just in the upper surface of the skin, and the infant grub at once tunnels inwards. Once well established underneath the hide, it makes a sort of chamber, where it lives its course, keeping the unlucky beast in which it dwells in a state of constant irritation and annoyance. The result is to set up an inflammation round the cell, which sometimes extends over a large surface on the animal's back. Sometimes there are evident signs of general illness, which, in very severe cases, may even lead to death; but, in the vast majority of instances, the only sign is the habit the animal indulges in of licking the affected place. In these cases the havoc wrought is not apparent until after slaughtering, when the hide reveals on its underside hollow pits, which open into holes in process of tanning. The carcase, moreover, is injured by the inflammation, which is the true cause of what butchers know as 'licked beef.' It is estimated that from one-quarter to one-third of the beasts which come to market in England are thus affected, to the great loss of the breeder and all concerned."

An instance is quoted in which 102,877 hides were passed through a market in twelve months, and 60,000 of them were warbled.

The loss on these hides alone is put down at £15,000.

Treatment.—Lay hold of the swelling between the finger and the thumb and squeeze out the grub, and inject some Phenyle and water, or Spirits of Camphor into the hole with a small syringe. This will thoroughly destroy the grub, and prevent many other cows from being affected by the insect.

17. HYDROPHOBIA.

Causes.—Bites from dogs, jackals, or other animals.

Treatment.—There is no treatment for this disease; the best thing to be done is to destroy the animal at once, but much may be done to prevent the disease.

Immediately an animal is bitten, bathe the wound with warm vinegar and water, and when this has dried, pour a few drops of *Muriatic acid* into the wound. This will destroy the poison of the saliva. Also give the animal the Mother Tincture of Belladonna, ten drops every morning and evening for a month.

18. HYDATIDS.—Tumours in the lungs or liver, sometimes in the brain, consisting of a sac lined by a thin bladder or cyst filled with a limpid colourless fluid; in this a number of cysts, from the size of a pea to an egg, are found floating.

Causes.—In India hydatids are caused from want of proper food and water, or starvation. The disease shows itself generally in the hot weather, when pasturage and water are scarce.

Symptoms.—The presence of the disease cannot be ascertained, but may be suspected from the following symptoms. Loss of appetite; suspension of rumination; dry muzzle, hot ears and horns, hurried breathing, rough, staring coat, rapid emaciation; sometimes there is no indication of disease except loss of flesh and general wasting.

Treatment.—Give the animal half a *seer* of rock salt (Sundhub lobon) pounded and dissolved in two quarts of warm water, with a quarter of a *seer* of powdered sulphur added to it, in the morning for a couple of days. After that give two *chittacks* of the salt every morning for a few weeks. Also give Arsenicum Alb. lx. or Phosphorus lx. ten drops every two or four hours.

Accessory Treatment.—Give the animal plenty of good wholesome food and pure water. The house should be clean, dry, and sweet.

19. Inflammation of the Bowels.

Causes. — Cold, chills, bad food and water, acrid substances, poisons.

Symptoms. — Shivering, hot skin, thirst, hard and frequent pulse; the pain becomes so severe that the animal tumbles down, turns its eyes about, and throws its head from side to side as if in great agony; the horns, ears, mouth, and feet become cold; breathing hurried; the animal will not allow its stomach to be touched. Mortification of the bowels sets in; death ensues.

Treatment.—At the commencement, Aconite Nap. is indispensable; give lx. ten drops every hour; then give Belladonna lx. or Dioscorea lx. ten drops every two hours. The stomach should be fomented with blankets, out of which hot water has been wrung.

An enema of two *seers* of hot water and four ounces of Glycerine should be given.

Accessory Treatment.—Keep the animal out of the draught, and give it only thin warm gruel.

20. HERNIA.—A large tumour protruding from the abdomen, caused by a rupture of the intestines.

For the proper treatment of this disease you need the services of a veterinary surgeon.

21. JAUNDICE is a symptom of disease generally affecting the liver, and not a disease itself.

22. POISONING.

Cattle die from poisons either accidentally taken with their food, or criminally given to them.

The poison may be either vegetable or mineral.

In parts of India cattle are poisoned by *chamars* so that they may obtain their hides. It is the custom generally throughout India to throw the carcases of cattle that die on the *bhagar*, and the hides are considered the perquisites of the *chamars* of the village.

In some districts *chamars* pay a rent to the zemindar for the right of taking the hides.

Chamars sell most of the hides to hide-merchants, and in many districts an agreement between the *chamars* and a hide-merchant is drawn up and signed, whereby the hide-merchant agrees to give so much money for a certain number of hides, provided they are supplied by the *chamars* in a given time; and it is customary for the hide-merchant to give some money in advance to the *chamars.*

This often leads to the *chamars* poisoning cattle in order to obtain a sufficient number of hides by the time mentioned in the agreement; and they have often been detected, either in giving the poison by their own hands to cattle, or employing their wives and children to administer it.

The common mode adopted is to mix the dose of poison with a little *ghi* or flour, wrap it up in a plantain or other leaf, and put it into the mouth of the bullock, or throw it on the ground in front of the animal when feeding, for him to eat up.

Another plan is to scatter the poison over a sweet bit of pasturage.

The third plan is to introduce the poison with a sharp instrument through the skin into any part of the body, or into the fundament or vagina.

The poison commonly used is one of the preparations of Arsenic, either white or yellow, generally the former;

sometimes vegetable poisons such as *Dhatura*, Aconite, *Madár*, and Nux Vomica are made use of.

It is believed that Arsenic is sometimes provided by the hide-merchant's agents, and given to the *chamars*.

Poisoning is probably often extensively carried on under the cloak of murrain, that is, when rinderpest is prevailing in a district more hides are secured by poisoning. Again, the *chamars* are well aware of the contagious nature of rinderpest, and an instance has been recorded of their having taken the contents of the stomachs and bowels of cattle that had died of the disease, to a distant village, where murrain had not prevailed, to scatter over the pasture-lands there, in order that the disease might be contracted by the cattle of the village, and they might have a new source of obtaining hides.

Cattle are sometimes poisoned by eating the castor-oil plant and seeds, and in seasons of drought, when pasturage is scarce, from eating acrid plants and herbage.

Symptoms.—When poisons are eaten by, or given to a bullock or cow in large doses, the symptoms are as follows: the animal becomes suddenly ill; seized with a trembling fit; most severe abdominal pain; striking the belly with the hind-legs or horns, and looking frequently round to the flanks; foams at the mouth; has great thirst; very often shows tetanic twitchings; signs of hoven; passes dung very often; diarrhœa sets in, and with it more or less blood is passed; generally, in from two to four hours death occurs, the time depending in a great measure upon the amount and kind of poison administered.

Treatment.—The dose of poison generally given is so large that treatment is seldom of use, and the antidotes are not at the hand of the cattle owners.

But if detected in time the following treatment may save the animal. Two quarts (or *seers*) of sweet oil (olive oil) or linseed oil poured down the animal's throat. Repeat the dose after an hour.

Accessory Treatment. — The diet should be linseed gruel, bran mash, and boiled *kullai*; but no grass or straw should be given for two or three days, after which soft *doob* grass may be allowed.

23. Abscess.—When an abscess forms on the udder, face, foot, or any other part of the cow's body, foment the part with boiled *neem* leaves and apply Belladonna liniment. This should be done twice or three times a day. Or else the Belladonna liniment should be applied, and then a linseed poultice put on the part. The poultice should be changed twice a day.

Five drops of Belladonna 1x. in a little water should be given to the animal twice a day. When ready, the abscess should be opened and the pus let out; after which it should be properly washed with Phenyle and water and dressed with Iodoform. It should be properly dressed twice a day.

CHAPTER IV.

CONTAGIOUS AND FATAL DISEASES.

1. RINDERPEST.

Names.—Boshonto (Bengali), gootee, matah (Hindi).

Rinderpest is a contagious fever of a typhoid type. It is the most contagious disease known. Under ordinary treatment, from 50 to 90 per cent. of cattle attacked die.

Causes.—Contagion: the time that elapses before an animal shows symptoms of the disease, after being exposed to contagion, is generally short, being from two to three days; but sometimes it appears in as short a time as twenty-four hours, and a rare instance has been recorded of it not having appeared before the twenty-first day.

Symptoms.—The first symptom is, increased temperature of the body; but this can only be tested by the use of a thermometer. The symptoms to be noticed by ordinary observers may be divided into three stages.

First Stage.—Dulness; shivering fit; coat staring; mouth hot; mucous lining of the mouth congested;

short husky cough; ears drooping; bowels generally constipated, and the dung coated with mucus; appetite partially lost; thirst often great; spasmodic twitchings of the muscles of the body, especially of the back, shoulders, or hind quarters; back arched, and the four legs drawn together; rumination slow and irregular; grinding of teeth; yawning; tenderness of the spine; pulse accelerated.

Second Stage.—Mouth, ears, horns, legs, and other parts of the body vary in temperature, being at one time hot, at another cold; respiration is much quickened; appetite lost; rumination ceases; slight discharge from eyes; increased tenderness of spine; lies down, with head turned back to the flank; fever high; thirst great; difficulty in swallowing; twitchings of muscles more marked; pulse very quick, but irregular; difficulty in moving; gums and buccal membrane and papillæ very red; tongue furred; bowels very costive, the pellets of dung coated with mucus and blood; lining membrane of rectum and vagina very red and dry; tenesmus; and occasionally prolapsus of rectum and vagina.

Third Stage.—Profuse discharge of very viscid mucus from eyes, nostrils, and mouth; very offensive breath, excoriations, coated more or less with yellow aphthæ, of gums, corners of the mouth, buccal papillæ, and roof and floor of the mouth and tongue, also sometimes inside the nostrils and eyelids; incisor teeth loose. Purging now sets in, the dung at first consisting of small hard pellets, covered with blood and mucus, and watery fæces, and afterwards of fluid matter only with flakes of mucus, blood, and aphthæ, and is most offensive in odour: occasionally emphysematous swelling under the skin. Great prostration; continued thirst, but greater difficulty in swallowing, followed by coughing, coldness of skin, horns, ears, legs, and mouth. Cows in calf generally abort. The animal lies down, indeed has not power to rise; moans, breathes with difficulty, grunts; liquid bloody fæces are involuntarily passed, the pulse is imperceptible, and death generally occurs in two to six days. Sometimes an eruption of the skin is seen about the dewlap, udder, groins, shoulders, and ribs; but this eruption is not by any means an invariable symptom, and when it occurs it is generally found in animals attacked in the hot season. This eruption is considered a favourable symptom, as, when it is profuse, dysenteric symptoms seldom prevail, and recovery often follows; when no eruption on the skin occurs, and violent dysenteric symptoms continue, death generally ensues.

The disease is not improperly considered by some native cattle owners a kind of small-pox. It is called *matah* by them when the eruption on the skin is evident, and is described as *andar-ka-matah* when the lining membrane of the stomach and bowels is so much affected as to lead to the passing of blood, mucus, and aphthæ.

In some cases, especially in those of rapid course, symptoms of delirium are shown by the animal becoming excited, and after plunging about, it will fall down, and become insensible and die.

If a cow is in calf, unless very great care is taken, she will slip her calf. Sometimes even with the greatest care this mishap cannot be prevented.

Treatment.—In India, treatment is often successful, and this may be attributed to the disease very often appearing in a mild form. Rinderpest belongs to a class of diseases which must run their course, that is, the poisonous material contained in the system must gain exit to allow of the patient recovering. The grand aim of the treatment should be to aid nature in ridding the system of the poisonous matter, and to support the strength of the animal by good care, nursing, and proper diet.

Ordinary Treatment.—Immediately the first symptoms appear give the animal two *chittacks* of Eno's Fruit Salt, or four *chittacks* of Epsom or half a *seer* of common salt in warm water, and repeat the dose every hour until the bowels are relieved.

When purging and passing of blood and mucus continue for more than twenty-four hours, give the following draught, which has proved successful in Mr. Thacker's hands:—

Camphor	$\frac{1}{4}$ tolah
Nitre (sora)	$\frac{3}{4}$ tolah
Dhatura seeds	$\frac{1}{4}$ kancha
Chiretta	$\frac{3}{4}$ tolah
Arrack	2 chittacks

But when the diarrhœa has existed above twenty-four hours, the following, finely powdered, may be added to the preceding prescription:—"Gall nut $\frac{3}{4}$ *tolah.*" This should be repeated every twelve hours until the purging ceases.

For sheep and goats one-sixth of the above dose should be given.

Native Treatment.—Fresh roots of the *chirchery* plant, four *tolahs*; fresh roots of the *jokha* plant, four *tolahs*; thorns of the *Shimul cotton* tree, four *tolahs.* Have the whole pounded or ground together very fine. Give a dose of twenty grains of this medicine three times a day for three days.

Ten grains for a dose to a calf, and five grains to a goat or sheep. All natives know the first and last-mentioned plant and tree, but *jokha* is the Santali name for a plant that grows wild in their district. The Bengali name of the plant is *Joyabâlta,* and the Hindi name is *Jukkha.*

Homœopathic Treatment.—As soon as the first symptoms are seen, give Aconitum Nap. lx. and Arsenicum Alb. lx.

ten drops alternately, every three hours; when the eruption appears, give Antimonium Tart. lx. one grain every three hours. If the eruption is driven in, give Spirits of Camphor, ten to twenty drop doses, every ten or fifteen minutes, until the skin gets warm and the eruption reappears. Sulphur is very good when the eruption is disappearing and there is great itching, etc.

If possible a doctor should be called in. I have found the native and the homœopathic treatment very effective.

Accessory Measures.—Immediately remove the sick animal from the rest of the herd. Until purging sets in, as much *cold* water as the animal will drink should be allowed it; but when purging sets in give *cold* water in small quantities. The diet must consist of rice and wheat or barley gruel, well boiled and of good consistency. Cool well, and give two *seers* three times a day. Nothing hot or warm must be given. Put some salt in the gruel. When the animal begins to get well, give it some fresh *doob* or soft green grass, besides the gruel. Hard, dry, fibrous food must on no account be given for some weeks after the creature has recovered. It may cause serious illness.

The mouth of the animal should be washed with a little warm water. It must be kept in a house, or room, free from draughts, but plenty of fresh air must be allowed the creature, and the room must be well ventilated. Nothing is of so much importance as pure air, and that in unlimited quantities.

If the skin seems very painful sponge the whole surface with warm water and Carbolic acid. If the cow is in milk and you let the calf drink the milk, the poor little thing is sure to get the disease.

The milk must be regularly extracted and buried. If the milk is not extracted from the cow, her udder will become very painful, and she will be in great distress.

All the dung and soiled litter must be immediately removed and the place kept perfectly clean.

Sprinkle some pure Carbolic acid mixed with hot water about the room.

Preventive.—The disease arises from contagion. Never let your cattle graze on the public roadside or run with outside cattle.

When the disease is prevailing in the district, give all your cattle a dose of that native remedy; or else a dose of Tincture of Sulphur, twenty drops every morning for three days.

2. Foot-and-Mouth Disease.

This disease is known by different names in different parts of India. The most common names are, *khoori* and *khoorpucha*.

It is a very contagious fever, accompanied with vesicular eruption in the mouth and feet and on the udder.

Sometimes the mouth only is affected, at other times the feet. In some cases the feet become first affected, in other cases the mouth.

It attacks cattle, sheep, goats, pigs, and fowls; and even man has become affected from drinking the milk of cows suffering from the disease.

It is constantly prevailing more or less in all parts of India.

An animal may suffer several times during its life from this disease.

Causes.—In the majority of cases the disease is caused by contagion, but it may be spontaneous in its origin, and then is probably due to the animal having been kept in a stall or ground in a filthy state.

Very often it is difficult to trace the cause, but it is scarcely ever found where cattle are kept in a clean state and by themselves, that is, not allowed to mix with other cattle or frequent highways; so the cause would generally appear to be due to contagion and want of cleanliness.

Experience proves that the period of incubation is from twenty-four hours to three or four days, but generally thirty-six hours.

Symptoms.—The symptoms first noticed are a shivering fit followed by fever, hot mouth, horns, and extremities, with smacking of lips and salivation. Then vesicular eruptions will be noticed in the mouth and feet, and in cows on the udder and teats. The eruption is like blisters of the size of a bean. These vesicles or blisters are sometimes seen on the nasal membrane; they burst in eighteen or twenty-four hours, and leave red sore spots, which either soon heal or turn into ulcers.

The tongue is chiefly affected, but the gums and roof of the mouth and the inside of the cheeks are in some cases also affected.

The eruption in the feet will be found at the junction of the skin with the hoofs, and between the hoofs.

From the mouth and feet being very sore, and the existing fever, the animal does not feed, and is very lame on the feet affected.

If the animal be a bullock and be kept at work, the symptoms will become more severe, the legs will swell, and very often the hoofs will be cast, and sometimes abscesses will form in the legs.

When the eruption is on the udder and teats, there will be swelling and tenderness of both.

If the milk of an affected cow be drunk by the calf or by man they will become affected.

In milk-cows, the teats often become very sore from the blistered parts being pinched by the hands of the milkman, and the udder sometimes swells and becomes inflamed from the milk not being drawn away.

The hands which milk diseased udders will carry the contagion to the udders of sound cows, if care is not taken to well wash the hands after milking an affected cow.

Goats and sheep are similarly attacked, but suffer in the feet most; when sheep and goats are afflicted they get much out of condition.

The disease is sometimes mistaken for rinderpest, but in foot-and-mouth disease, as found in India, purging is not one of its symptoms, whereas diarrhœa and dysentery are invariable accompaniments of rinderpest. Again, in rinderpest the feet are not affected.

It is possible for an animal to have at the same time both rinderpest and foot-and-mouth disease, but such a case is rarely met with.

If an affected animal is properly cared for, all symptoms of fever will disappear in three or four days, and the animal will be well in ten or fifteen days with little loss of condition; but if care is not taken of the animal, and in the case of bullocks, if made to work, the fever will become severe, the appetite less, and from the ulceration extending between the hoofs and the feet, the hoofs may drop off; the legs will become much swollen, and abscesses will form in them, death occurring in ten or twelve days.

When the cattle are large and heavy, they suffer more from this disease than lighter and smaller cattle.

In some attacks the disease is mild, in others, of a severe type.

In India, the percentage of deaths among those attacked ought not to exceed two or three per cent., and with common care an animal rarely dies from this disease.

Ordinary Treatment.—Wash out the mouth two or three times a day with warm water, and afterwards with—

Alum	1 chittack
Warm water	½ seer

Wash and foment the feet with warm water and soap twice a day, carefully removing all dirt, especially from between the hoofs, and dress the sores with—

Mustard oil	¼ seer
Turpentine	2 chittacks
Camphor	2 chittacks
Phenyle	½ chittack

The udder, teats, and other parts affected with sores, should be kept clean and dressed frequently with the above-mentioned dressing, which will prevent flies blowing the sores and breeding maggots. If the flies attack the mouth the camphorated oil should be applied to the mouth twice a day.

When there is much fever, give the following twice a day:—

Camphor	¼ tolah
Nitrate of Potash	3 tolahs
Arrack	½ chittack
Water	4 chittacks

Homœopathic Treatment.—As soon as the least sign of the disease is discovered, give Arsenicum Alb. lx. in ten drop doses every three hours. Separate the animal from others.

If the disease has properly set in, give Arsenicum Alb. lx. and Belladonna lx. ten drops, alternately, every two hours.

Wash the mouth first in clean warm water, then in the following:—

Alum	1 chittack
Warm water	½ seer

Wash the feet and udder twice or thrice a day in warm water, with soap, and apply this ointment—

Mustard oil	¼ seer
Turpentine	2 chittacks
Camphor	2 chittack
Phenyle	½ chittack

or else the following:—

Warm water	½ seer
Phenyle	1 chittack

Accessory Measures.—The animal must ke kept housed and clean, and the floor of the house must be kept scrupulously clean, and the house or room thoroughly ventilated. Give the animal plenty of fresh air.

Doob, or some soft green grass and rice gruel, with an

ounce of salt and three ounces of treacle, must be given to the creature twice or three times a day.

Sprinkle pure Carbolic acid and water or Phenyle and water about the room.

Preventive. — The disease, in the majority of cases, arises from contagion. Adopt measures recommended in Chapter I.

Give Arsenicum Alb. lx. ten drops every morning while the disease is prevailing in the district.

3. Malignant Sore-throat.

This is a fatal and very contagious disease. Calves are very liable to get it.

Causes.—Blood-poison, caused by impure air and water; infection; bad feeding; bad housing. (See Chapter I.)

Symptoms.—The first symptoms often are those of influenza; loss of appetite; suspension of rumination; cough; discharge from the nose and mouth and eyes; fever; inflammation of the lining of the nostrils and eyelids; swelling of the throat and glands below the ears and between the jaws; swelling of the tongue and the back part of the mouth; difficulty in swallowing and breathing; breath becomes very offensive; diarrhœa; the tongue protrudes from the mouth and is dark in colour, ulcerated, and has purple patches on some parts. The head is protruded, and there is great weakness.

The symptoms rapidly increase, and the animal dies from suffocation in from one to two hours, or two or three days.

Treatment.—The best thing to do is to at once destroy the animal and have it buried far away from the house, six feet underground. If the animal be a very superior one, you may at once separate it from the others, and try the following treatment. This disease is similar in character to diphtheria. Give Belladonna ϕ, and Mercurius Iodatus lx., five to ten drops, or one grain, alternately, every two or three hours. Wash the mouth and nose with Condy's Fluid or a lotion of Carbolic acid.

Baptisia ϕ, and Arsenicum Alb. lx., alternately, ten drops every two hours, should be given if the above remedies do not effect any improvement.

Accessory Treatment.—The house and everything connected with the animal must be kept perfectly clean Barley, wheat, or corn gruel must be given to the animal in small quantities frequently; a tablespoonful, or a small wineglassful of brandy must be given with the gruel, if there be extreme weakness. A hot bath may do the animal much good, but a blanket must be kept over it after the bath. Free ventilation in the room and cold water to drink are very necessary.

In severe cases the doctor will open the windpipe, and thus may save the animal. The meat, skin, urine, and dung of the diseased animal are very poisonous, and all should be buried.

4. Bronchitis from Cold.—This is a very dangerous disease, and is infectious.

Causes.—Exposure to wet or cold, or to sudden changes of temperature; a neglected cold or catarrh; contagion.

Symptoms.—The symptoms at first are those of a common cold, and afterwards seem to be similar to those of sore throat; the cough at first is very dry and has a grating sound; there is a mucus discharge from the nose and the mouth; the cough becomes very painful and frequent; the countenance appears anxious and distressed; the breathing is quick and heaving and obstructed, in consequence of accumulation of tough, tenacious phlegm; there is unwillingness to move; the breath is hot; the cough is increased by moving about; no food is eaten; the animal wastes, and the skin becomes dry and bound to the ribs; coat stares and looks unhealthy; death ensues. It may end in inflammation of the lungs.

Treatment.—The animal must be kept in a warm but well-ventilated room. Give Aconite Nap. lx. and Bry. Alb. lx. alternately, ten drops every two hours.

When there is inflammation of the eyelids, and a discharge from the eyes and nose of a watery kind, give Arsenicum Alb. 1x. ten drops every two hours, alternated with Aconite.

When the discharge from the eyes and nose is of a mattery character, and the supply of milk is scanty, give Mercurius Sol. 1x. or Mercurius Iod. 1x. one grain every two hours, alternately with Aconite.

The following liniment must be well rubbed into the throat, chest, and sides: —

Mustard oil	4 chittacks
Spirits of Turpentine	4 chittacks
Camphor	1 chittack

In severe cases the chest must be fomented with flannel and hot water, or a bran or linseed poultice must be put on the chest and sides.

Accessory Treatment. — Keep the animal perfectly clean and warm and quiet. Give it wheat, barley, or corn gruel, in small quantities (one quart) frequently. The gruel should be warm.

Water should be given in small quantities occasionally.

No grass, straw, or leaves must be given for some days.

5. Bronchitis from Worms. — This also is a very dangerous and infectious disease. Calves and yearlings, and young goats and sheep, are specially subject to it.

Causes. — Small worms of a silvery white colour in

the windpipe and its branches, caused by impure water and food, or insufficient supply of pure water; worms in the water, grass, or grain; impure air; over-crowding. If one animal is affected, then many more of the same herd will be attacked, if preventive measures are not adopted.

Symptoms.—There is a slight discharge from the nostrils, and a dry, husky cough, which becomes most violent and comes on in fits; the animal is dull and drooping, and quickly loses flesh; there is much distress in the chest, and the animal grunts often; goats and sheep cry out as if in great pain; a thin discharge flows from the nose; loss of appetite; great weakness; as the disease increases, the symptoms become more severe, and death follows in a few weeks.

Treatment.—Loss of time and neglect of the premonitory symptoms will prove fatal. The only thing to be done is to detach and expel the worms. This may be done by one of the following remedies.

(1) Pour one teaspoonful of chloroform down each nostril of the animal; a less quantity must be given to smaller animals.

This treatment has proved successful in many cases.

(2) Put from a dram and a half to two drams of Phenyle in one ounce of water, and pour gently down the throat. Do this twice a week until cure is effected. Half the quantity for small calves, or goats and sheep.

(3) Mix thoroughly, and give every second or third day. Half the quantity for small calves, goats, and sheep.

Turpentine	1 chittack
Spirits of Camphor	80 drops
Castor oil	4 chittacks
Phenyle	¼ dram

Accessory Treatment.—The affected animal must have one *chittack* of sulphur and four *chittacks* of salt every day in its food, or with a little gruel before its food. It should have lots of gruel and bran mash, but dry, hard food should not be allowed.

The affected animal must be separated from the rest, and sulphur must be burned in the room, so that it can inhale the fumes.

Preventive.—Cleanliness in food and drink; regular supply of salt and sulphur in the food; sufficient food and water; separation from the affected ones.

6. SCARS.—These scars are seen about the throat or neck. They look like cancers, but they do not kill.

As long as there is a slight discharge from the sore, the cow keeps in good health, but as soon as the discharge is checked, she goes off her food and gets out of sorts; the part where the sore is swells, and a running at the mouth, nose, and eyes, and sometimes looseness of the bowels set in.

This disease is not contagious, but calves and men drinking the milk of cows thus affected will also get the disease.

Treatment.—Give Arsenicum Alb. lx., or Fowler's Solution of Arsenic, ten drops every four hours for a month. Wash the sores with Phenyle and water, but the sores should not be allowed to close up suddenly.

Preventive.—Sufficient salt and sulphur in the food.

7. ANTHRAX.—Called black-quarter, congestive fever, gloss-anthrax, splenic apoplexy, etc.

This is a blood disease, and in India is contagious, though in cold climates it is believed not to be so; it is generally accompanied with a swelling under some part of the skin, generally on the loins, or hind or fore quarters, or throat and sometimes tongue. The swelling is puffy and crackles when pressed upon by the hand.

The disease has been found to be communicable to other animals and to man in the form of malignant pustules.

Causes.—When cattle, which have been for some time kept on very poor, bare, or reedy pasture, are put on rich grazing grounds, they become very often affected; the younger cattle are specially liable to become affected, as in them blood is more rapidly formed than in older animals. The blood not only becomes suddenly enriched, but also vitiated, and escapes from its vessels in those soft parts of the body loosely connected. The most thriving animals are the most susceptible, especially those which are rapidly improving after having been in somewhat low condition. Again, at seasons when cattle are not sheltered at night, and the days are very hot, and the nights cold, they are more liable to become affected.

In certain badly drained lands in Great Britain, the disease was wont to occur frequently; but since the lands have been properly drained, the disease is seldom met with. In some parts of the continent of Europe, the disease is always more or less present at certain seasons, on lands where the drainage is defective.

Doubtless, in India, outbreaks of black-quarter frequently depend upon cattle pasturing on marshy lands.

When one head of a herd is attacked, it is almost certain that others will also become affected, not merely from contagion, but also on account of having been probably fed and cared for in a manner similar to the one ill.

Symptoms.—The attack is generally very sudden. An animal, seen perfectly well a short time before, may be found in an hour or two afterwards to be dull and stiff, and to have a difficulty in moving, and in a few minutes a swelling will be observed under the skin in some part of the body, generally on the loins, hind quarters, fore quarters, or throat and tongue. Sometimes the disease may be located in the chest or abdomen, or even brain.

When the swelling under the skin is examined, it is found to crackle under the pressure of the fingers, and to feel as if blown out with air; but this is owing to gas generated by the rapid decomposition of the blood. If the throat and lungs are principally involved, then the breathing will be distressed; if the brain is affected, there will be symptoms of stupor, and when the spleen and other parts of the abdomen become gorged, signs of abdominal pain will be evident.

The disease though sudden may be preceded by dulness and listlessness. The patient loathes food, but may be thirsty at first and drink greedily; rumination ceases; the ears, horns, and muzzle are hot and dry; breathing is hurried, with expanded nostrils and open mouth; breath hot; flanks heaving; and constant moaning is observed. The pulse, full and excited at first, becomes weak and tremulous; subsequently, the animal is disinclined to move; the neck and head are extended, eyes protrude and are congested; the animal may become unconscious or insensible; when induced to move, it staggers and is lame in both hind quarters, constantly drooping on either to obtain ease; it tumbles down and makes vain efforts to rise. These symptoms increase in severity, and the animal dies of exhaustion in twelve, eighteen, or twenty-four hours.

Treatment.—In the first stage of the disease give Ammonium Causticum lx. and Aconite Nap. lx. alternately, ten drops every half or quarter of an hour.

If the above-mentioned medicines effect no improvement in an hour and a half, or only partial improvement, then give Belladonna ϕ and Aconite lx. alternately, ten drops every hour.

When the hind quarters are much affected and there is much lameness, give Bry. Alb. lx. with Aconite or Ars. Alb. alternately, every half-hour; when there is much weakness give Arsenicum Alb. lx. with Bry. Alb.

Foment the parts swollen with flannel and hot water, and if there be any sores, wash them with Arsenic and water.

Wash the mouth with cold water constantly.

Accessory Treatment.—Keep the animal well sheltered and give it lots of pure water to drink; mix a quarter of a *seer* of common salt, quarter of a bottle of Eno's Fruit Salt, and one *chittack* of Flower of Sulphur in a quart of warm water, and give it to the creature twice a day. Give it no food for a day or so; on the second day only thin gruel should be given. Rice or barley gruel is the best.

Preventive.—When one of a herd is attacked, others will have a tendency to become affected; it is therefore advisable to adopt preventive measures. Give the animals a quarter of a *seer* of salt every day, and plenty of pure cold water to drink. Protect them from sudden changes of weather. Keep them on bare grass, green, soft, and fresh.

The lands must be properly drained, and dirt and offensive matter at once removed from near the place.

Inserting a seton in the dewlap of each animal has proved a most successful preventive measure. Also give each animal Arsenicum Alb. lx. ten drops every morning.

The same treatment will do for goats and sheep.

8. DYSENTERY.—Inflammation of the lining membrane of the large intestines, sometimes accompanied with ulceration. It is contagious.

Causes.—Neglected diarrhœa; eating unwholesome grass or plants; drinking bad water; exposure to severe cold or damp at night, or excessive heat in the day; feeding upon marshy or badly drained lands; overwork or driving; sudden stoppage of milk; sudden disappearance of skin eruption; want of good and sufficient food: contagion.

Symptoms.—Shivering fit; skin hot: dulness: anxiety: hair slightly rough; uneasiness: pain in the abdomen: straining; passing blood and pus with the dung; the animal wastes, and loses appetite and spirits; sometimes the dung is dry and in small lumps, but generally the discharge is watery and attended with severe pain; the rectum may become everted; sometimes the skin and mouth become yellow; the animal wastes away.

Treatment.—Give Mercurius Corrosivus 1x. five drops every two hours. Keep a blanket round the stomach and abdomen. If the purging be excessive give Arsenicum Alb. 1x. ten drops every two hours alternately with Mercurius.

Accessory Treatment.—Give rice gruel. It must be given in small quantities frequently. Take a good large ripe bail, break it, and scoop out all the inside with a spoon. Take one and a half to two *seers* of water; put the bail in the water and dissolve thoroughly. Remove the seed and strings from the stuff. Give two bottles of this twice a day. When ripe bail cannot be had, take an unripe one and roast it in the fire for a few minutes. When the dung hardens give rice and linseed gruel. No grass or leaves must be given for some time. Keep the animal clean and dry and in a clean, dry, and well-ventilated house; if the night be cold, put a blanket over the animal.

9. Blain.—A fatal and contagious disease.

Causes.—Impurity of the air; poisonous herbs; taking into the body some of the discharge from the diseased animal's mouth.

Symptoms.—The cow is low-spirited, dull, and does not eat, nor chew the cud; a clear fluid, without smell, flows constantly from the mouth; the head and neck gradually swell until they are much increased in size; difficult breathing; the fluid from the mouth becomes mattery or mixed with blood, and smells very disagreeable; the tongue swells and its sides are covered with blisters, which at last burst and become sores. Fever sets in; the whole of the tongue swells and mortifies; death ensues. The disease runs its course sometimes in a few hours. Cattle, goats, sheep, and even men are liable to the contagion.

Treatment.—Open the blisters as early as possible, and wash the mouth with Carbolic acid and water, or Condy's Fluid and water, three times a day.

Give Mercurius Iodatus lx. five grains, and Belladonna ϕ ten drops, alternately every hour or two.

Accessory Treatment.—Keep the animal away from the others in a clean and well-ventilated shed; keep the creature's mouth and body perfectly clean.

Give it rice, linseed, barley, or gram gruel in small quantities frequently. If the animal cannot drink, pour the gruel down its throat through a drench-horn or bottle. No grass or other food should be given.

Preventives.—Keep the healthy animals away from the sick. Fumigate the shed, and everything connected with it, with sulphur: also sprinkle and wash the place well with Carbolic acid (pure) and water. Great care must be taken lest the other animals or the keeper get any of the discharge from the diseased animal into their mouth, nose, eyes, or upon a sore on the body.

10. SLINKING OR ABORTION—Bringing forth the calf before the proper time. The cow generally slinks between the fifth and eighth month after conceiving. Abortion is contagious.

Causes.—Blows, falls, strains, jumps, severe exertion, forcible movements, and other injuries; rinderpest, hoven, internal inflammation; eating certain herbs that grow on marshy or badly drained lands; drinking dirty water or water impregnated with iron; intercourse with the bull during pregnancy; exposure to bad smells, arising from rotten matter, especially if it be the cleansing of a cow that has just slinked—in this case, the cow is said to abort from "sympathy"; over-feeding during pregnancy, over-heating food or insufficient food; fright.

Symptoms.—One has to be very observant to notice the symptoms that warn of the approach of the mishap. Unless proper means are adopted at the first appearance of danger, there is no chance of averting it. The symptoms are dulness; loss of spirits; want of appetite; loss of cud; hollow flanks; enlargement of the lower part of the belly; disinclination to move; unsteady walk; the calf does not move at the flanks; breathing laboured; a yellowish discharge from the vagina; the belly continues to fall; fever sets in; the animal moans; the calf is expelled at last. It is either already dead or lives only a short time.

Treatment.—If the discharge from the vagina is fetid, then it is sure the calf is dead, and the sooner it is expelled the better. Give Pulsatilla 1x. ten drops, every hour until it is expelled.

If the calf is alive, do all you can to prevent the miscarriage. Give Secale Cor. 1x. ten drops, or one grain, every six hours. Pour cold water over the loins and haunch.

If the abortion is actually taking place, then give Secale Cor. 1x. ten drops every fifteen minutes.

If the discharge of blood be bright red, give Sabina 1x. the same as Secale. When the abortion is caused by blows, falls, and injuries, give Arnica Mon. 1x. ten drops, as Secale.

Accessory Treatment.—Remove the cow from the others, and keep her quiet in a clean and well-ventilated room. Give her light and sloppy food, and pure cold water. The dead calf and the after-birth and every trace of the abortion must be buried deep underground far from the other cows.

11. GONORRHŒA.—A contagious disease.

Causes.—Want of cleanliness; repeated acts of coition: sexual intercourse with a diseased animal; the discharge, or the water the diseased animal has been washed in, touching the animal.

Symptoms.—In the cow the disease shows itself in from two to five days after sexual intercourse. The first symptoms are, constant shaking and side movement of the tail, which sometimes is kept close over the fundament; the vagina gradually becomes very sore and much swollen, and red inside; a mattery discharge flows; the urine is made in small quantities and frequently accompanied with much pain.

In the bull, the sheath is red and swollen, a discharge of matter issues from it; the urine is made in small quantities and comes out in jerks, and is attended with much pain.

Treatment.—Keep the parts perfectly clean. Wash with soap and water and inject the following into the part.

Five grains of Argentum Nitricum to a pint of distilled water, injected three times a day, or twenty drops of Tincture of Iodine to a pint of water, injected three times a day.

Give internally Mercurius Sol. lx. and Cantharis lx. one grain or ten drops, alternately, four times a day.

Preventives.—Remove the diseased animal from among the healthy ones, and also all soiled straw, earth, etc., and wash the place thoroughly with Phenyle or Carbolic acid and water.

12. COW-POX.—This is a contagious disease, but is not

fatal, except in cases of gross neglect. It is an eruptive fever, and attacks animals only once in a lifetime.

Cause.—Generally, infection.

Symptoms.—Eruptions about the centre and base of the teats and sometimes on the udder itself in the form of circular pustules, which, when fully formed, attain the size of a four-anna bit. The disease may show itself and run its course followed by some constitutional disturbance without detection, except in the instance of milk-cows.

The pustules are generally situated on the udder and teats, and irritate milk-cows so that they become restless and violent during the process of milking. The pustules are of a circular form, with its centre depressed and margins raised and filled with a clear fluid, which gradually becomes opaque and purulent, and is surrounded by a red blush of inflammation. In the course of a few days the pustules burst and scabs form; the scabs dry and fall off in a fortnight or three weeks. Sometimes the udder swells up very much and is painful; the cow will not allow the calf to suck, nor will she allow herself to be milked. Unless great care is taken, the milk will dry up and the cow will be utterly spoiled. Sometimes the animal has small lumps all over her, and under her skin they are so soft as not to be felt by the hand, but they give the coat a rough, lumpy look.

Treatment.—Separate the animal at once. Wash the affected parts with *warm* water and smear with fresh butter or *ghee.* Every drop of milk must be extracted. If there be any difficulty in doing this, then tie the cow's hind-legs together, and place a pot of hot water under the udder and steam it, or, better still, wash the udder with warm water and a sponge; do not make the water hot, or else you will injure the udder. When the udder becomes soft, wipe it dry with a clean dry cloth, and rub it over with butter or *ghee.* Then commence to milk her, but be careful not to press the fingers on the pustules. Thus you may extract all the milk. The cow must be treated with great tenderness and care.

Give the animal Aconite 1x. and Arsenicum 1x. alternately, ten drops every four hours. When the udder swells and is painful give Belladonna 1x. instead of Arsenicum.

Accessory Treatment.—Keep the animal in a clean, dry, and thoroughly ventilated room, and feed it on light sloppy food. Withhold everything indigestible.

13. Milk Fever.

Milk or Puerperal Fever is a very dangerous and infectious disease. It generally attacks the best and fattest cows. Some say that more than 75 per cent. of the cows attacked die. This may be true under other methods of treatment, but I have found homœopathy to be very successful in the treatment of this disease, and the death-rate is not at all great.

Causes.—Over-feeding before and immediately after calving, in order that the cow may produce a large quantity of milk; sudden change of weather; exposure to cold or wet; driving the cow a long journey; contagion. Some cows are more subject to it than others.

Symptoms.—The disease generally shows itself from the third to the fifth day after calving. Sometimes the disease begins on the first day. The cow refuses her food, or eats very little of it; she is depressed, hangs her head, and looks dull; the horns are hot; the nose is hot and dry; the urine is scanty; bowels are confined, or the dung is hard and lumpy; the pulse is quick and full; the breathing is quickened, and the flanks heave. *In the second stage* the milk is reduced or nearly stopped; the eyes glisten, and look bright and staring; the white of the eye is covered with red streaks, or it is of a leaden colour; the cow looks anxious and weak; the hind-legs seem weak and are set apart from each other; she is restless and uneasy; she does not chew the cud; all discharge from the bearing is stopped; the calf is neglected; the pulse becomes slow, and the breathing more difficult; the udder becomes hard and swollen, and there is great difficulty in drawing out the milk. *In the third stage* the cow gets startled; the breathing becomes more hurried, and the flanks heave much; the mouth opens, and saliva flows from it; the animal staggers and falls, the body begins to swell, the extremities grow cold; there is shivering, with cold perspiration; she struggles, as if in great pain; death ensues.

Treatment.—At the first appearance of any of the symptoms, give Aconite lx. and Belladonna lx. alternately, ten drops every hour or half-hour. Continue the above remedies in the second stage. In the third stage, give Arsenicum Alb. lx. and Ammonium Causticum lx. alternately, ten drops every fifteen or twenty minutes.

When improvement sets in and the bad symptoms have subsided, give Nux Vom. lx. and Bry. Alb. lx. alternately, ten drops every hour or two. In the first stage of the disease give the animal half a bottle of Eno's Fruit Salt, and four *chittacks* of common salt, in one *seer* of warm water. If this does not act on the bowels, then give the same quantity in a second dose, an hour after the first. I have found Eno's Fruit Salt a very beneficial remedy.

Every drop of milk must be extracted three or four times a day. The calf should not be allowed to drink the milk. Rub Tincture of Aconite on the udder.

Accessory Treatment.—Keep the cow in a dry, cool, and thoroughly ventilated room; the open air is preferable to a close room. If the body is very hot, throw a blanket over her. Give her some warm rice, wheat, or kullai gruel three or four times a day, also warm water to drink.

No grass or other food should be allowed until the symptoms subside. Keep the room and the animal perfectly clean. Wash the vagina two or three times a day with warm water. If the discharge from the vagina smells bad, inject some Condy's Fluid and warm water into it.

Preventive.—The disease is contagious.

When two or more cows calve at the same time or within a week of each other, keep them apart. Keep newly calved cows away from the affected animal. Avoid the causes mentioned above. Wash the vagina with warm water. If a cow is subject to it, give her a dose of Eno's Fruit Salt in warm water twenty-four hours after calving, and Aconite 1x. and Belladonna 1x. alternately, ten drops every two or four hours for three days.

14. Worms in the Intestines.

There are three principal kinds of parasites that invade the intestines of cattle, goats, and sheep. There may be more than the three kinds mentioned, but these three are the principal ones.

They are (1) the small thread-worm, (2) the long round-worm, (3) the tape-worm. The thread-worm is from a quarter to one inch long, of a silvery white colour, and often exists in clusters or balls, chiefly, but not exclusively, in the rectum.

The long round-worm is very much like the common earth-worm, but nearly white, and measures from six to eighteen inches or more. They never exist alone.

The tape-worm often exists alone, and measures from three inches to many yards in length.

I have seen the thread-worm and the long round-worm in the same animal at the same time, and once I found the long round-worm and the tape-worm existing in the same stomach.

Causes.—Impure water and food. Worms in the water and food will be sure to cause the disease. Young calves suffer from it when they are over-fed with milk; swallowing flies will cause it. Infection. If one animal in the herd or flock has got worms, the rest are likely to be infected also. The worms travel and enter the anus, or are swallowed in the food.

Symptoms.—The only certain proof of the presence of worms is the detection of the creatures themselves, or their ova, in the dung, or in what is thrown out when the animal coughs. But the following are some of the symptoms noticed in the infected animal:—A short, dry cough; eating or licking of mud; diarrhœa; loss of appetite; rough, staring coat; dropping of the ears; grinding the teeth; pain in the stomach; wasting; passing of slime, and sometimes worms.

Treatment.—The treatment I have found most effective is the following:—

Immediately you detect the least symptoms of worms in the intestines, give the animal the following:—

Spirits of Turpentine	2 drams
Spirits of Camphor	40 drops
Castor oil	3 ounces
Phenyle	½ dram
Sulphur	½ ounce

Mix the whole thoroughly, and pour it down the throat gently. The above dose is for a small calf or a goat or sheep; for a larger animal double the quantity. The dose should be repeated every four days or week, until the worms die, and are passed out in the dung. When the worms are dead, stop the above medicine and give four ounces of Eno's Fruit Salt in a pint of warm water, early in the morning; fifteen minutes after the salt is given give the animal two quarts of linseed gruel, thin and warm, and keep it tied up for half an hour or an hour; if during that time it is not purged, then give it a second dose of the same quantity of gruel. Repeat for three or four days.

Give double the quantity to large animals. Unless the dead worms are expelled from the stomach the animal will die.

When you find the animal will not eat, it must be fed by pouring rice or linseed gruel down its throat.

After the animal has been purged and the worms passed out, give it a dose of the condition powder (see *Recipes*) every morning for a few weeks, and feed it on soft sloppy food.

Accessory Treatment.—Keep the animal perfectly clean and warm, free from wet and cold winds. Keep the house and utensils perfectly clean. Remove the dung immediately it is dropped, and change the litter every morning; the soiled litter should be burned. Give the animal plenty of pure drinking-water, fresh, soft green grass and bran and oilcake mash. The bran must be steeped in boiling water first. Small calves, kids, and lambs should be given warm skimmed milk and rice or linseed *kanji*. Keep the diseased animal apart from the rest.

Preventive.—Absolute cleanliness, and sufficient salt and sulphur in the food, and pure drinking-water.

15. PLEURO-PNEUMONIA.—This is a disease of the lungs and the lining membrane of the chest. It is a contagious disease; is peculiar to cattle, goats, and sheep, affecting all breeds, at all ages, at all times, and in all climates. It is most insidious in its attack, sometimes rapid and sometimes protracted in its course, varying from one week to four months, or even a longer period. It does not, as a rule, attack every head in a herd; indeed, it is capricious in the way it spreads.

Causes.—It is found to exist in low, damp, ill-drained, and badly ventilated shippens; in swampy, damp, fenny districts, in which various gases, the products of vegetable decomposition, are given off, and become mixed with the air which the cows breathe. It prevails most frequently at certain seasons of the year, and when the weather is undergoing some change, and is damp and chilly; or when a sudden change from heat to cold, or the reverse, occurs. Some cows are more liable to be attacked than others; thus it is far less frequent, fatal, or difficult to cure in country districts than in towns or large shippens near towns, where the animals are living in a highly artificial manner, being crowded together, highly fed, and milked dry, in order to increase the quantity of milk. This unnatural mode of life peculiarly fits the cow to be acted upon by any of the exciting causes. Many persons consider the disease to arise from some peculiar condition of the atmosphere, akin to that which produces cholera and influenza in human beings. It is, moreover, contagious—that is, the disease is propagated from diseased to healthy cows by contact or contiguity.

The best proof of it being caused, as it is now generally believed to be, by contagion is, that in certain stocks in Great Britain, where the disease has not occurred, all the cattle of these herds have been home-bred and kept isolated from other cattle—that is to say, no stock is ever introduced, but all is home-bred. Wherever pleuro-pneumonia is met with, the affected cattle have been so situated as to be exposed to contagion, and a careful inquiry will prove that such has been the case.

The period of incubation of this most insidious disease is from ten days to three or even more months.

Symptoms.—The first symptoms noticeable by a professional man are, increased temperature of the body, and other signs by auscultation and percussion, but the symptoms to be recognised by cattle owners will be only detailed.

The first symptom is that of the animal looking perhaps better than usual; indeed, having perhaps improved somewhat in condition; and this state will continue for a few days, when perhaps the attendant will notice the animal to have a shivering fit, and the pulse will be found to have increased; the mouth hot, muzzle dry; cough, the cough being of a peculiar husky kind; loss of appetite; and, if a milch-cow, a less supply of milk.

In a day or two symptoms of fever set in, the coat stares, the mucous membranes are much injected, the mouth is very hot, and the breath is no longer sweet; the cough becomes worse and is painful, and there is increased difficulty of and rapidity in breathing; the pulse is very quick and full, numbering from 80 to 100; but after a time it becomes small and weak. The nose is poked out, in order to render breathing as easy as possible, but every respiration is attended with a grunt; the nostrils are very much dilated, and the breathing is rapid; when standing the animal turns out the elbows, and when lying down lies on the centre of the chest-bone, so as to cause expansion of the chest; or if only one side of the chest is affected, the animal will generally lie inclining to that side, so as to give every facility for breathing with the sound lung on the other side. Occasionally, symptoms of hoven are seen; a slight discharge from the eyes and nose generally occurs; the extremities, horns, and skin become cold, and the breath very offensive.

The cough then becomes more frequent, but is not given with any force; it has been well described as a "*masked cough*"—in other words, a cough that the animal cannot give with force, and therefore it sounds as if purposely checked with the view of preventing much noise. The skin becomes very dry and hide-bound; the animal has gradually lost condition, but is now becoming emaciated.

Pressing the fingers between the ribs gives pain, and the animal grunts or moans. In the latter stage of the disease purging sets in. After the fever (which is invariably more or less present in all cases) subsides, the animal recovers appetite, and throughout the disease is found to eat fairly, or even well; but as the disease continues so do the lungs become more and more closed and heavy, the breathing more difficult, and the blood is no longer duly purified; so gradually emaciation follows, and ultimately the animal dies from suffocation.

In favourable cases, the disease affects only a portion of the lungs or only one lung, and the animal apparently recovers, but remains in poor condition.

In many cases, the disease so runs its course as to involve both lungs to an extent which leads to suffocation and death.

Duration.—The duration of the disease will depend upon the nature of the attack; if severe and rapid in its course, death will result in a week or ten days; if of a mild and protracted type, death may not occur for two, three, or even six months.

In India, though it is often protracted in its course, it is generally fatal, as the disease is seldom noticed until it has firm hold of the system.

Treatment.—We cannot too strongly impress upon every cow-owner the importance and necessity for his own sake of noticing particularly when the *first symptoms* of this disease show themselves, for at this time it is quite manageable; and if every cow had the remedies given as soon as she became affected, very few, if any, would die. The timely discovery of the first symptoms of the malady, and the administration of the appropriate remedies, would very considerably lessen the fatality of the disease, and be an immense saving to every owner.

In many cases which the author has treated, the cows were quite well within a few hours after the disease began; the medicine checked it at once, and permanently.

The following are the remedies which have proved the most efficient: Aconitum, Bryonia, Arsenicum, Ammonium Causticum, Phosphorus, and Sulphur. Now these medicines are to be chosen and used according to the following directions.

Let us take an illustration: Supposing a person has a cow ill of this disease, he must ascertain the state of the pulse, its character—whether hard or soft—and its frequency; as to the condition of the breathing, whether quick, panting, or difficult; attended with pain and grunting or not: as to the chewing of the cud and the giving of milk; and, in short, as to the presence of all the other symptoms or sufferings which he can find out in the animal as indicative of pleuro-pneumonia. Having done so, let him read the following remarks carefully:—

1. If his cow is affected in the following way: Pulse hard and quickened; breathing short, painful, anxious, attended with groans, and open mouth; burning dryness of the mouth; shivering or trembling, attended with cold skin, especially of the legs, and followed by dry heat of the entire surface: then he must give the cow Aconitum 1x.

Dose.—Ten drops in a wineglassful of water, given

every one, two, or three hours, according to the violence of the symptoms just mentioned.

2. If the cow is suffering from these evidences of the complaint: Frequent, short, suppressed cough, which conveys to a looker-on the idea that the action of coughing causes sharp pain in the chest, and the cow tries to lessen this by stopping or cutting short the effort of coughing. For the same reason the breathing is short, attended with pain and the characteristic grunt; pain followed by flinching and grunt when the ribs are pressed against; the animal remains standing in one place, and is unwilling to move, because the pain in the chest would be thereby increased: then he must give the cow Bryonia 1x.

Dose.—The same as the last medicine.

3. If the cow is ailing in this way: Quick, difficult breathing, attended with rattling sound; the breathing inwards is short, in consequence of pain; cough frequent and attended with discharge of phlegm from the wind-pipe; great weakness, listlessness, and depression; pulse feeble and quickened; frequent shivering or trembling; skin hot and dry, afterwards moist: then choose Ammonium Causticum 1x., and give it in the same way as directed for Aconitum.

4. If the symptoms are these: Wheezing, short and difficult breathing; small, quick pulse; great weakness and loss of appetite; grinding of the teeth; cold skin

and clammy sweats; frequent short cough; purging, either in first or last stage: then Arsenicum lx. is the most suitable, and it must be given as directed for Aconitum.

5. If the following symptoms exist: Breathing difficult, oppressed, and obstructed; pains in the chest, which are aggravated by taking a deep breath, by moving about, and by coughing; pain between the ribs; frequent short cough, attended frequently with the discharge of slimy phlegm, which is sometimes mixed with blood: then Phosphorus lx. is required, and must be given as directed for Aconitum.

6. Sulphur vi. exerts its beneficial action in this complaint, more especially when one or other of the foregoing remedies have subdued the more violent symptoms, and when the cow is slowly recovering. Its chief effect seems to be to confirm the tendency towards health, and to guard against a relapse.

Dose.—Ten drops in water, or on a little bread, three times a day.

Accessory Treatment. — When an animal becomes affected, it must be carefully housed and nursed; the house should be well ventilated and kept perfectly clean, so as to ensure an abundant supply of pure air. Hot-water fomentation should be applied, and the animal kept warm.

The diet must be of green grass and other soft and

laxative food, such as wheat and rice kanjee, and pure water *ad libitum*. Rank dry grasses or straw should not be given.

It must be remembered that the disease will often prove to be incurable; but when an animal does recover, the constitution will be often found permanently weakened. Unless the animal is taken in hand in the first stage of the disease there is no chance of recovery.

Whenever the disease attacks an animal, it should be at once isolated and kept apart from all other cattle, and the persons attending the sick beast should not attend the sound cattle. If the disease is far advanced, it is best to destroy the animal and have it buried at a distance, six feet under ground.

Post-mortem Appearances.—The lungs of a healthy ox are light, and do not weigh more than five or six pounds. When a bullock dies from pleuro-pneumonia, the lungs will be found heavy, and when cut into, liver-like or mottled, and containing here and there pus in cysts, and will weigh from thirty to thirty-seven pounds; they will be also found more or less attached to the sides of the chest.

In some cases only one lung will be affected.

RECIPES.

1. To Destroy Maggots.—Spirits of Camphor poured into the wound, or, custard-apple leaves and camphor ground together and put into the wound. Close up the mouth of the wound with lint. Wash thoroughly every morning and evening with Phenyle and warm water.

2. Horn-oil.—Mustard oil, half *seer*; bees-wax, half *chittack*; camphor, one *chittack*.

3. Hoof-oil.—Tar, one *chittack*; camphor, one *chittack*; bees-wax, one *chittack*; mustard oil, four *chittacks*; and turpentine, one *chittack*.

4. Purifying Water.—Quarter of a teaspoonful of powdered alum in a *ghara* of water.

5. How to Administer Medicine.—Give the medicine on a small piece of dry bread, or else make a bamboo tube (*chonga*), or take a long-necked strong bottle, put

the medicine in it, make a man hold the animal by the horns, take hold of the creature by the mouth, raise its head up to the level of its back, open the mouth, hold down the tongue with the thumb of the left hand, introduce the *chonga* or bottle into the mouth and pour in a little of the medicine; as soon as it has swallowed it, more must be given, until the whole is taken. The drench-horn is preferable when at hand.

Care should always be taken, especially in animals suffering from sore throat, in giving the medicine in small quantities at a time, and if the animal coughs, or attempts to cough, the assistant should at once let go the head so as to allow the animal to depress the head and cough freely, and thereby prevent the chance of any of the medicine passing into the windpipe. If the assistant does not let go the head as soon as there is any sign of the animal wishing to cough, some of the medicine may pass into the windpipe and cause death.

6. SETON.—Make a cut three-fourths of an inch in length through the skin with a sharp knife, and another cut through the skin of the same size two or three inches distant; pass some plaited horse-hair, or string, with a large needle, through the one cut, along under the skin, to and through the other cut; then tie the two ends of the plait in a firm knot, but so that the loop may not press upon the skin between the two incisions.

Dress the seton and neighbouring skin three or four times a day, with Phenyle and water or Carbolic acid and water, to prevent the flies blowing the part and to increase the action of the seton.

Passing a seton in the dewlap is simply done by pushing a sharp needle, threaded with the plaited string, through the dewlap.

7. CONDITION POWDER, or tonic for horses, cattle, sheep, and goats.

Black salt	½ seer
Sulphur	½ seer
Dried ginger	½ seer
Chiretta (powdered)	½ seer
Camphor	¼ seer
Ajwain (Bishop seed)	½ seer
Mustard seed	½ seer
Mathee	½ seer
Turmeric	½ seer

All to be well powdered and mixed together. From ¼ to ½ *chittack* to be given to each animal every morning and evening. Half the quantity for goats, sheep, and calves. Continue for a month.

It should be given with the food or else in some *suttoo*, or given in half a quart of water as a drench.

8. BELLADONNA LINIMENT—

Tincture of Iodine	1 ounce
Spirits of Camphor	1 ounce
Extract of Belladonna	1 ounce
Glycerine	½ ounce
Alcohol	1½ ounce

all properly mixed together. To be applied to the affected part with a camel's-hair brush.

9. Gruels.—One *seer* of gram, wheat, rice, barley, or linseed well ground and mixed with four or five *seers* of water and properly boiled for an hour and a half, a dessert-spoonful of salt added.

10. Poultices.—Linseed poultice—grind the linseed into powder, mix some in hot water and place over a fire; stir well until it thickens; place on a thick piece of cloth, and put it over the affected part.

Bran to be so mixed in hot water as to form a soft paste; place on a cloth, pour a little common oil over the upper surface, and apply. Should the wound be very unhealthy, sprinkle powdered charcoal or sugar over the poultice before applying it to the wound, and change the poultice and charcoal frequently. Wash the wound with hot water thoroughly before putting on a fresh poultice.

11. Fumigation.

Shed.—Burn sulphur (gondhok) in an iron spoon over fire in the cow-house with partially closed doors for half an hour, or until the gas causes the animals to cough.

Single Animal.—Burn sulphur or tar in an iron

vessel over fire in front of the bullock or cow, so that the fumes may be inhaled by the animal.

In fumigating, care is necessary so that the animal may be able to inhale air as well as the smoke of the sulphur or tar.

The inhaling of the fumes of sulphur and tar alone, without being mixed with a sufficiency of air, would kill an animal.

12. Fomentation.—Apply for from a quarter to half an hour very hot water with a flannel or *kombol* cloth, taking care that the part fomented is not chilled; then thoroughly dry the part with dry cloths, and rub in—

Mustard oil	4 parts
Oil of Turpentine	2 parts

well mixed together.

13. Disinfectants.—Phenyle, one part to ten of water. Pure Carbolic acid, one part to eight of water. Quicklime, sprinkled over the floor, and smeared over the walls. They also destroy vermin.

14. Vermin Destroyer.—Besides the above, the following is very effective: Dry tobacco leaves and catechu soaked in water, and the floor, walls, and wood well rubbed with it.

To apply to the bodies of animals, Phenyle and water, and Keating's insect-powder, or the following preparation, are the safest remedies :—

Mustard oil	8 chittacks
Spirits of Turpentine	4 chittacks
Gum Camphor	2 chittacks
Flower of Sulphur	4 chittacks
Phenyle	1 chittack

15. HOMŒOPATHIC MEDICINE should be given in water. Quarter of a pint of water for each dose of medicine.

HOMŒOPATHIC MEDICINES.

For the convenience of the reader, I here subjoin a list of all the remedies prescribed in this book. The medicines can be obtained from any Homœopathic chemist at a small cost. The proper thing to do, is to have all the medicines put up in two small chests, one for internal use and the other for external use. The medicines should be always at hand for immediate use. There should be a third box for ordinary remedies.

MEDICINE CHEST, No. 1.

INTERNAL REMEDIES.

One-ounce bottles.

1. Aconite Napalis lx. ϕ.
2. Ammonium C. lx.
3. Antimonium Tar. lx.
4. Arnica Mon. lx. ϕ.
5. Arsenicum Alb. lx.
6. Baptisea ϕ.
7. Bryonia Alb. lx.
8. Belladonna lx. ϕ.
9. China Off. lx.
10. Cantharis lx.
11. Dioscorea lx.
12. Euphrasia lx.
13. Gelseminum S. lx.
14. Hepar Sulp. 3x.
15. Mercurius Cor. lx.
16. Mercurius Ioda. lx.
17. Mercurius Sol. 3x.
18. Nux Vomica lx.
19. Pulsatilla Nig. lx.
20. Phosphorus lx.
21. Rhus Tox. lx.
22. Sabina lx.
23. Secale lx.
24. Silicea 6x.
25. Sulphur lx.

MEDICINE CHEST, No. 2.

EXTERNAL REMEDIES.

Four-ounce bottles.

1. Aconite ϕ.
2. Argentum N. ϕ.
3. Arnica M. ϕ.
4. Belladonna ϕ.
5. Calendula Off. ϕ.
6. Hydrastis C. ϕ.
7. Rhus Tox. ϕ.
8. Glycerine.

MEDICINE CHEST, No. 3.

One-pound bottles.

1. Spirits of Camphor.
2. Condy's Fluid.
3. Eno's Fruit Salt.
4. Epsom Salt.
5. Glycerine.
6. Phenyle.
7. Spirits of Turpentine.
8. Flower of Sulphur.
9. Tincture of Iodine.
10. Alum.
11. Iodoform.
12. Belladonna liniment.
13. Linseed oil.
14. Castor oil.
15. Condition powder.

ϕ means the strong tincture known by Homœopathic chemists as Mother Tincture.

No. 77.

TELEGRAMS:
"MOFUSSIL, LONDON."

ESTABLISHED 1816.

A

CATALOGUE

OF

RECENT AND FORTHCOMING

PUBLICATIONS

ISSUED BY

W. THACKER & CO.

2, CREED LANE, LONDON, E.C.

AND

THACKER, SPINK & CO.

CALCUTTA AND SIMLA.

1898.

LIST OF AUTHORS.

RUDYARD KIPLING.
CAPT. M. H. HAYES, F.R.C.V.S.
L. G. CARR LAUGHTON.
CAPT. L. J. SHADWELL, P.S.C.
HENRY O'BRIEN.
M. MOOKERJEE.
VERO SHAW.
JOHN WATSON, F.L.S.
E. MARKWICK.
FRED T. JANE.
VETY.-MAJOR J. A. NUNN, F.R.C.V.S
E. H. AITKEN.
LINCOLN SPRINGFIELD.
HAMLIN GARLAND.
D. C. BOULGER.
W. LAIRD CLOWES.
H. G. KEENE, C.I.E.
J. G. WHYTE MELVILLE.
PAUL CUSHING.
GENERAL KINLOCH.
MAJOR W. YELDHAM.
H. E. BUSTEED, M.D., C.I.E.
ALFRED E. PEASE, M.P.
H. S. THOMAS, F.L.S..
E. D. MILLER.
LADY VIOLET GREVILLE.
MRS. O'DONOGHUE.
COL. H. M. S. BRUNKER.
DANIEL BRUNN.
THACKER'S INDUSTRIES OF INDIA.
" INDIAN DIRECTORY.
;, MAP OF INDIA.
Surgn.-Capt. C. H. BEDFORD, D.Sc., M.D.
EDWARD A. BIRCH, M.D.
J. B. LYON.
Surgn.-Major S. TARLETON YOUNG.
Col. H. L. THUILLIER.
T. W. JONES.
W. J. WILKINS.
JOGANDRA NATH BHATTACHARYA M.A., D.L.
GEORGE ABERIGH-MACKAY.
R. A. STERNDALE.
KANNY LALL DEY, C.I.E., F.C.S.
"SNAFFLE."
Lieut.-Col. R. H. TYACKE.

SPORT

Crown 8vo., Cloth, Gilt Top, 6/-

Hunting Reminiscences.

BY

ALFRED E. PEASE, M.P.

Author of "The Cleveland Hounds as a Trencher-fed Pack," "Horse-breeding for Farmers," etc.

WITH ILLUSTRATIONS BY THE LATE SIR FRANK LOCKWOOD, CUTHBERT BRADLEY, HEYWOOD HARDY, AND FROM PHOTOGRAPHS.

CONTENTS.—The Cambridge Drag and House of Commons Steeplechase. The Life of a Hunter. Hounds. Hare-Hunting. Fox-Hunting. Badger-Hunting. Cub-Hunting. The Greatest Run I ever saw, etc.

Also an Edition de Luxe, limited to 200 numbered copies at one guinea net, beautifully printed from newly-cast type on Dickinson's hand-made deckled-edge paper, and the Illustrations printed on the finest art plate paper. In addition to this the size of the book is enlarged to demy 8vo., giving wider margins to the pages, and there are several extra Illustrations not included in the smaller edition.

"There is more to be learned from Mr. Alfred E. Pease's little volume of 'Hunting Reminiscences' than from a library of more pretentious treatises. The frontispiece is a portrait of the author himself on a favourite mare. But where he really paints himself is in every page, and long before we have got to the concluding chapter we seem to know him intimately as we like him much. Mr. Pease, like Sol Gills, is 'chockful of science,' but there is not a touch of pedantry in his manner of imparting his knowledge—the reader picks it up incidentally as he goes galloping along, for the pace is good from the start to the finish."—*Times.*

Crown 8vo., Cloth Gilt, 6/-

Riding Recollections and Inside the Bar.

BY

J. G. WHYTE MELVILLE.

WITH ILLUSTRATIONS BY HUGH THOMSON.

Also an Edition de Luxe, (limited to 200 numbered copies) printed on Dickinson's hand-made paper, with extra Illustrations, in Demy 8vo., handsomely bound, One Guinea net.

"When the late Sir Charles Knightley took Sir Marinel out of training and brought him down to Pytchley, to teach him the way he should go (and the way of Sir Charles over a country was that of a bird in the air) he found the horse restive, ignorant, wilful, and unusually averse to learning the business of a hunter. The animal was, however, well worth a little painstaking, and his owner, a perfect centaur in the saddle, rode him out for a lesson in jumping the first day the hounds remained in the kennel. At two o'clock, as his old friend and contemporary, Mr. John Cooke, informed me, he came back, having failed to get the rebel over a single fence. 'But I have told them not to take his saddle off,' said Sir Charles, sitting down to a cutlet and a glass of Madeira; 'after luncheon I mean to have a turn at him again!'"

SPORT.

Crown 8vo. Cloth, 3/6.

Notes on Stable Management in India and the Colonies.

BY

Vety.-Major J. A. NUNN, F.R.C.V.S.

SECOND EDITION, revised and enlarged, with a Glossary.

CONTENTS.—Food, Water, Air, and Ventilation, Grooming, Gear, etc.

"Soldiers and others about to leave England for the East for the first time should not fail to possess themselves of a copy of this work. They can read it on the voyage, and find themselves all the better for the instruction conveyed by the time they reach the other side."—*Field.*

Crown 8vo. Sewed, 1/6.

How to choose a Dog and How to select a Puppy.

With Notes on the Peculiarities and Characteristics of each Breed.

BY

VERO SHAW.

(Author of "The Illustrated Book of the Dog." Late Kennel Editor of the "Field.")

"Each breed of dog has a chapter to itself which opens with a few introductory remarks of a general nature; then follow the points briefly and plainly; next come average of the pup from six weeks old until he attains maturity. A couple of pages at the end of the work are devoted to the relation, and a few useful hints on buying, feeding, and breeding. Needless to add that like all Mr. Vero Shaw's writings on canine subjects the information is founded on practical experience and imparted in easy excellent English."—*The Stock Keeper.*

Demy 4to., handsomely bound, 42/-

Large Game Shooting

IN

Thibet, The Himalayas, and Northern India.

BY

Brigadier-General ALEXANDER A. KINLOCH.

Containing Descriptions of the Country and of the various Animals to be found, together with Extracts from a Journal of several years' standing.

Third Edition, with 34 beautiful Illustrations and a Map of the District.

"The splendidly illustrated record of sport. The photogravures, especially the heads of the various antelopes, are lifelike; and the letterpress is very pleasant reading."—*Graphic.*

SPORT.

CAPT. HAYES' BOOKS ON HORSES.

Super-Royal 8vo., Cloth, Gilt Top, 34/-

Points of the Horse.

A familiar Treatise on Equine Conformation.

BY

Capt. M. HORACE HAYES, F.R.C.V.S.

SECOND EDITION. Revised and enlarged.

This Edition has been thoroughly revised and contains numerous additions, including specially written Chapters on the Breeds of English and Foreign Horses.

Illustrated by 200 reproductions of Photographs of Typical "Points" and Horses, and 205 Drawings by J. H. OSWALD BROWN.

"A year or two ago we had to speak in terms of praise of the first edition of this book, and we welcome the second and more complete issue. The first edition was out of print in six months, but, instead of reprinting it, Capt. Hayes thought it better to wait until he had enough material in hand to enable him to make to the second edition those additions and improvements he had proposed to himself to add. The result is in every way satisfactory, and in this handsome book the searcher after sound information on the make and shape of the horse will find what will be of the utmost use to him. Those who have been, or who contemplate being at no distant date, in the position of judges at horse shows, will derive great benefit from a careful perusal of Capt. Hayes' pages."—*Field.*

Thick Crown 8vo., Buckram, 15/-

Veterinary Notes for Horse-Owners.

An Illustrated Manual of Horse Medicine and Surgery, written in simple language, with over 200 Illustrations.

BY

Capt. M. HORACE HAYES, F.R.C.V.S.

FIFTH EDITION.

Revised throughout, considerably enlarged, and incorporates the substance of the Author's "Soundness and Age of Horses."

"Of the many popular veterinary books which have come under our notice, this is certainly one of the most scientific and reliable. If some painstaking student would give us works of equal merit to this on the diseases of the other domestic animals, we should possess a very complete veterinary library in a very small compass."—*Field.*

SPORT.

Imperial 16mo., Cloth Gilt, 10/6.

Riding: on the Flat and Across Country.

A Guide to Practical Horsemanship.

BY

Capt. M. HORACE HAYES, F.R.C.V.S.

"We are not in the least surprised that a third edition of this useful and eminently practical book should be called for. On former occasions we were able to speak of it in terms of commendation, and this edition is worthy of equal praise."—*Field.*

Crown 8vo., Cloth, 6/-.

Training and Horse Management in India.

BY

Capt M. HORACE HAYES, F.R.C.V.S.

FIFTH EDITION.

"We entertain a very high opinion of Capt. Hayes' book on 'Horse Training and management in India,' and are of opinion that no better guide could be placed in the hands of either amateur horseman or veterinary surgeon newly arrived in that important division of our empire."—*Veterinary Journal.*

Imperial 16mo., Cloth extra, 12/6.

Modern Polo.

A Practical Guide to the Science of the Game, Training of Ponies, Rules, &c.

BY

Mr. E. D. MILLER, late 17th Lancers,

Edited by Capt. M. H. HAYES, F.R.C.V.S

WITH SIXTY-FOUR ILLUSTRATIONS FROM PHOTOGRAPHS.

"***How to become a Polo Player.***—A good horseman, whose eye has been educated by such games as cricket and racquets, and who thoroughly understands football or hockey, the tactics and combinations of either of which greatly resemble those of polo, will not take long to master the peculiarities of polo, and ought to be a really good performer after three months of regular play. Here, as in all other games which demand quickness of eye and skill of hand, assiduous and long-continued practice is imperative. At first glance it may appear strange to say that many men play polo well in spite of being bad horsemen. Hence the fact that a man knows little about riding should in no way deter him from giving the game a trial."—*Vide page* 3.

SPORT.

Imperial 16mo., Buckram, 21s.

Illustrated Horsebreaking.

BY

Capt. M. HORACE HAYES, F.R.C.V.S.

SECOND EDITION.

This Edition has been entirely re-written; the amount of the letterpress more than doubled, and 75 reproductions of Photographs have been added.

"It is a characteristic of all Capt. Hayes' books on horses that they are eminently practical, and the present one is no exception to the rule. A work which is entitled to high praise as being far and away the best reasoned-out one on breaking under a new system we have seen."—*Field.*

Infective Diseases of Animals.

Being Part I. of the Translation of Friedberger and Frœhner's Pathology of the Domestic Animals.

Translated and Edited by Capt. M. H. HAYES, F.R.C.V.S.

Author of "Points of the Horse," etc.

WITH A CHAPTER ON BACTERIOLOGY BY DR. G. NEWMAN, D.P.H.

In Two Vols. medium 8vo., 12s. 6d. Net each Vol. When completed the work may be had bound two vols. in one, price 25s. Net.

"Owing to the fact that the infective diseases of animals can in many cases be communicated to man, and that their occurrence in our meat and milk producers is a serious question of public hygiene, the present portion of this translation will appeal to doctors as well as to veterinary surgeons. The second part which I hope to have ready before long, will, of course, more particularly concern the veterinary profession." *Vide Preface.*

. . *Syllabus of Contents* . .

INFECTIVE DISEASES.

Septicæmia and Pyæmia. Malignant Oedema. Petechial Fever. Strangles. Canine Distemper. Bovine Malignant Catarrhal Fever. Epizootic Abortion. Dysentery. Swine Erysipelas. Swine Fever. Chicken Cholera. Wildseuche. Quarter-ill. Equine Influenza. Equine Contagious Pleuro-pneumonia. Tuberculosis. Actinomycosis. Equine Stomatitis Pustulosa Contagiosa Diphtheritic Diseases. Parasitic Stomatitis. Tetanus. Glanders. Bovine Contagious Pleuro-pneumonia. Dourine. Aphthæ. Anthrax. Rabies. Foot and Mouth Disease. Rinderpest. Texas Fever. Relapsing Fever. Surra. Cape Horse Sickness, etc.

CHRONIC CONSTITUTIONAL DISEASES.

Anæmia and Chlorosis. Pernicious Anæmia. Hydræmia. Leucæmia. Hæmophilia. Scurvy. Gout. Diabetes Mellitus. Diabetes Insipidus Obesity. Sarcomatosis and Carcinomatosis. Scrofula.

SPORT.

Square 8vo., Cloth Gilt, 10/6.

The Horsewoman.

A Practical Guide to Side-Saddle Riding.

BY

Mrs. HAYES. Edited by Capt. M. H. HAYES.

With 4 Collotypes from Instantaneous Photographs, and 48 Drawings after Photographs, by J. H. OSWALD BROWN.

"This is the first occasion on which a practical horseman and a practical horsewoman have collaborated in bringing out a book on riding for ladies. The result is in every way satisfactory, and, no matter how well a lady may ride, she will gain much valuable information from a perusal of 'The Horsewoman.' The book is happily free from self-laudatory passages."—*Field.*

Foolscap 8vo., Cloth, 6/-

The Sportsman's Manual.

In Quest of Game in Kullu, Lahoul, and Ladak, to the Tso Morari Lake.

BY

Lieut.-Col. R. H. TYACKE.

(Late Her Majesty's 98th and 34th Regiments.)

With Notes on Shooting in Spiti, Bara Bagahal, Chamba, and Kashmir, and a detailed description of Sport in more than 100 Nalas. With 9 Maps.

Crown 8vo, Cloth, 8/6.

Seonee.

Or, Camp Life on the Satpura Range. A Tale of Indian Adventure.

BY

R. A. STERNDALE.

Author of "Mammalia of India," "Denizens of the Jungles."

ILLUSTRATED BY THE AUTHOR.

With a Map and Appendix containing a brief Topographical and Historical Account of the District of Seonee in the Central Provinces of India.

Crown 8vo., 6/-.

The Snaffle Papers.

BY

"SNAFFLE."

Author of "Gun, Rifle and Hound," "In the Land of the Bora," "In the Jungle, &c."

A series of Sporting Sketches, embracing English and German Sportsmen—Old Coaching Days in the Lake District—Twenty Years of Polo—On the use of Buckshot—Game Laws of Europe—Japanese Deer—Shooting Ladies—Wild Bosnia—The Hazel Grouse, etc., etc.

NAVAL AND MILITARY.

Crown 8vo, Cloth, 12/-

A Text Book of . . Indian Military Law.

BY

Capt. E. H. BERNARD, Cantonment Magistrate, Mandalay

Comprising the Indian Articles of War fully annotated, the Indian Penal Codı and the Indian Evidence Act, and has, in the form of Appendices, all existin Regulations with regard to the Procedure of Courts-martial and Forms of Charges With Tables showing the Powers and Jurisdiction of different Courts-martial, and tha difference in Procedure and Evidence between English Military Law and India Military Law.

"A well-arranged and clearly printed Manual . . . . . with ample notes marginal references and appendices. . . . Every officer in India should possess copy of this handy compilation."—*Home News.*

Crown 8vo, 5/-

Indian Articles of War.

BY

Major C. E. POYNDER.

Revised to date. With an Appendix containing Definitions, Rules of Procedure Forms of Charges, Statement of Objects and Reasons and an Index.

"The annotations are very good, and we commend the volume to all concernee in the Military Legal Procedure of India."—*Army and Navy Gazette.*

Oblong Folio, Cloth Gilt, 10/6.

A New Work on Torpedoes.

The Torpedo in Peace and War.

BY

FRED T. JANE.

Author of "Blake of the Rattlesnake," "All the World's Fighting Ships," "The 'Jane' Naval War Game," &c.

WITH FULL-PAGE AND SMALLER ILLUSTRATIONS BY THE AUTHOR.

HISTORY AND TRAVEL.

Two Vols., Demy 8vo., 24/-

The History of China.

BY

D. C. BOULGER.

Author of "Chinese Gordon," "Sir Stamford Raffles," etc., etc.

A NEW EDITION REVISED AND BROUGHT UP-TO-DATE.

With the Recent Concessions to the European Powers.

Illustrated with Portraits and Maps.

"The Chinese, like the Jews and the ancient Egyptians, alone claim to trace back their national existence to a period centuries before Solomon erected his temple or Homer collected the ballads relating to the Trojan war and turned them into his immortal epic. From a date anterior to that accepted for the occurrence of the flood of Noah, the people of China possess a history which preserves the names of kings and conquerors, and describes remarkable events with an appearance of exactitude that would almost compel credence. In comparison with their institutions those of ancient Egypt and Assyria have only moderate claims to antiquity, and the states of Greece and Rome were but the creations of yesterday. The observer might well stand aghast, if he were called upon to follow the exact details in the history of a people and an empire which were great and definite in form nearly five thousand years ago."

Demy 8vo, Gilt Top, 12/6 Net.

Third Edition of O'Brien's Round Towers of Ireland.

Edition limited to 750 numbered copies, and the type distributed.

The Round Towers of Ireland,

Or the History of the Tuath-de-Danaans for the first time unveiled.

BY

HENRY O'BRIEN, B.A.

With all the original Illustrations, to which is added a portrait of the Author, reproduced from Maclise's well-known drawing.

This new edition contains all that is to be found in the previous editions, including the curious preface, together with valuable supplementary matter comprising an Introduction, a minute Synopsis of the Work, and a copious Index. It may be added that the text of the original has not been subjected to any alteration or modification, even its paging being preserved

The first edition of this work was published so far back as 1834, and a second edition was issued the same year.

No standard work on the Round Towers of Ireland has given rise to so much controversy as O'Brien's. To readers interested in Archæology and kindred subjects this new edition will doubtless present many advantages owing to its completeness.

The early editions having long been out of print, copies of the work are very scarce, and when they occur for sale, usually fetch from 35/- to 40/-.

HISTORY AND TRAVEL.

Demy 8vo.,

The Congo State;

Or the Growth of Civilization in Central Africa.

BY

D. C. BOULGER.

Author of "History of China," "Chinese Gordon," etc.

[IN THE PRESS.

Two Vols., Crown 8vo, 15/-

The Mayo College.

"The Eton of India."

A Record of Twenty Years, 1875 to 1895.

BY

HERBERT SHERRING, Headmaster.

"In these volumes on 'The Eton of India' the author has, besides giving a full and detailed account of the Mayo College, compiled biographies of Lord Mayo and the different Viceroys who have ruled India since the inception of the institution together with brief accounts of Rajputana, the Rajputs, the feudatory States, and some two hundred or more of the leading families of the Province. The credit of originating the scheme for securing to the sons of the aristocracy of India a liberal and enlightened education seems to belong to the late Colonel Walter, who, in the Bhartpur Agency Report of May 28, 1869, warmly advocated the establishment of an institution which should make clear to the Chiefs of India that our object was to perpetuate their dynasties by placing within their reach better facilities for the education of their sons than they could formerly obtain. 'Then,' he writes, 'and not till then, can we hope to see the native princes of India occupying the position they ought to hold as the promoters of peace, prosperity, and progress among their own people, and the hearty supporters of British authority and power.'"—*Morning Post.*

Demy 8vo., Cloth,

The Cave Dwellers of Southern Tunisia.

BY

DANIEL BRUNN.

Translated from the Danish with numerous Illustrations.

[IN THE PRESS

FICTION.

Crown 8vo, 6/-

A Galaxy Girl.

A New Novel.

BY

LINCOLN SPRINGFIELD.

"One would welcome a dozen such chapters as the one headed, 'A permanent object lesson to gamblers.' There is no clumsiness, no indecision, in Mr. Springfield's workmanship. His style is clean and correct, his humour is natural, and he has a grip of human nature and a skill in the contrivance of plot and exciting incident which give the impression that, admirable though this novel is, it gives only an indication of his fullest possibilities as a writer of popular fiction."—*Daily Mail.*

Cloth Gilt, 3/6

The City of Gold.

BY

EDWARD MARKWICK.

WITH 8 ILLUSTRATIONS BY HAROLD PIFFARD.

"It is really interesting and exciting."—*Daily Telegraph.*

"A succession of surprising adventures."—*Morning.*

Crown 8vo., 6/-

The Shepherdess of Treva

A New Novel.

BY

PAUL CUSHING.

Author of "The Blacksmith of Voe," "I' Th' Thorn," etc.

"Mr. Cushing has achieved a very great success in 'The Shepherdess of Treva.' "—*Academy.*

FICTION.

Crown 8vo., Cloth, 6/-

Wayside Courtships.

BY

HAMLIN GARLAND.

"'Wayside Courtships' is without a doubt a book to be read, and its author is a writer to be watched. We have not had such a welcome American arrival since the introduction of Miss Wilkins."—*To-Day*

"Where so much is good it is an ungrateful task to linger unduly over faults of styles and taste. I have read 'Wayside Courtships' with keen pleasure, and I warmly recommend the work to my readers. The two prose poems 'At the Beginning' and 'The End of Love is Love' are pregnant with the beauty closely akin to the mystical silhouettes in Olive Schreiner's 'Dreams.'"—*Critic.*

"It would be difficult to decide in which of the many beautiful characteristics lies the chief charm of these brief sketches. The keen observing powers of the author have resulted in the presentation of equisitely natural scenes which are vividly pictured by a skilful pen."—*Liverpool Mercury.*

Crown 8vo., Cloth, 6/-

Rose of Dutcher's Coolly.

BY

HAMLIN GARLAND.

"The author of 'Rose of Dutcher's Coolly' scores a marked success, chiefly, as it seems to us, because he has written his book to please himself, and with no attention to rigid rules of form or to the conventions of modern fiction. The book is the spontaneous outcome of a man's mind—a thing much more rare now than in the days when the novelist's art was in its infancy. . . . The outcome of this and of his talent is a book striking, orignal, and throughout distinguished above the ordinary. . . . We wish the book the success it deserves; and in congratulating the author on his achievement, we desire to add a word of congratulation to the publishers, for the get-up of the book is as excellent as its matter."—*Pall Mall Gazette.*

Crown 8vo, Cloth, 6/-

Jason Edwards.

And a Little Norsk.

BY

HAMLIN GARLAND.

Author of "Wayside Courtships," "Rose of Dutcher's Coolly," "A Spoil of Office," "A Story of the Modern West," "A Member of the Third House," etc.

INDIA.

Crown 8vo, Cloth, Gilt, 6/-

Lays of Ind.

Comical, Satirical, and Descriptive Poems illustrative of Anglo-Indian Life.

BY

Major W. YELDHAM ("ALIPH CHEEM").

ILLUSTRATED BY THE AUTHOR, LIONEL INGLIS, AND OTHERS.

TENTH EDITION.

"The 'Lays' are not only Anglo-Indian in origin, but out-and-out Anglo-Indian in subject and colour. To one who knows something of life at an Indian 'station' they will be especially amusing. Their exuberant fun at the same time may well attract the attention of the ill-defined individual known as 'the general reader.'"—*Scotsman.*

Crown 8vo., Cloth Gilt, 6/-

The Tribes on my Frontier.

An Indian Naturalist's Foreign Policy.

BY

E. H. AITKEN.

WITH FIFTY ILLUSTRATIONS BY F C. MACRAE.

SIXTH EDITION.

"This is a delightful book, irresistibly funny in description and illustration, but full of genuine science too. . . There is not a dull or uninstructive page in the whole book."—*Knowledge.*

Crown 8vo., Pictorial Cloth, 6/-

Behind the Bungalow.

BY

E. H. AITKEN.

Author of "Tribes on My Frontier."

FIFTH EDITION. ILLUSTRATED BY F. C. MACRAE.

"There is plenty of fun in 'Behind the Bungalow,' and more than fun for those with eyes to see. These sketches may have an educational purpose beyond that of mere amusement; they show through all their fun a keen observation of native character and a just appreciation of it."—*The World.*

INDIA.

Crown 8vo, Cloth Gilt, 6/-

A Naturalist on the Prowl.

BY

E. H. AITKEN.

Illustrated by a series of 80 Drawings by R. A. STERNDALE, F.R.G.S., F.Z.S., Author of "Mammalia of India," "Denizens of the Jungle," "Seonee," etc., who has studied and sketched animals of all kinds in their habitat and at work.

SECOND EDITION.

"It is one of the most interesting books upon Natural History that we have rea for a long time. It is never dull, and yet solid information is conveyed by nearl every page."—*Daily Chronicle.*

Post 8vo., Cloth Gilt, 7/6.

Echoes of Old Calcutta.

A most interesting series of Sketches of Calcutta Life, chiefly towards the close of the last century.

BY

H. E. BUSTEED, M.D., C.I.E.

THIRD EDITION, carefully revised and enlarged, with additional Illustrations.

"It is a pleasure to reiterate the warm commendation of this instructive ane lively volume which its appearance called forth some few years since. It would be lamentable if a book so fraught with interest to all Englishmen should be restricted to Anglo-Indian circles. A fresh instalment of letters from Warren Hastings to his wife must be noted as extremely interesting, while the papers on Sir Phillip Francis Nuncomar, and the romantic career of Mrs. Grand, who became Princess Benevente and the wife of Talleyrand, ought by now to be widely known."—*Saturday Review.*

12mo., sewed, 2/-

Onoocool Chunder Mookerjee.

A Memior of the late Justice Onoocool Chundeı Mookerjee.

BY

M. MOOKERJEE.

FIFTH EDITION.

"The reader is earnestly advised to procure the life of this gentleman, written by his nephew, and read it."—*The Tribes on My Frontier.*

INDIA.

Demy 8vo., Cloth, 12/-

A Servant of 'John Company.'

(THE HON. EAST INDIA COMPANY.)

Being the Recollections of an Indian Official.

BY

H. G. KEENE, C.I.E,, Hon. M.A. (Oxon).

Author of "Sketches in Indian Ink," etc.

WITH A PORTRAIT IN PHOTOGRAVURE.

Illustrated by W. SIMPSON *from the Author's Sketches.*

"Mr. Keene has written an instructive book. He is not dull. This book presents a novel view of Indian life. It is the genial record of a man who from boyhood seems to have bent on extracting the largest possible amount of pleasure from his surroundings."—*Times.*

Demy 8vo., Cloth, 15/-

The Rod in India.

Being Hints how to obtain Sport, with remarks on the Natural History of Fish and their Culture.

BY

H. S. THOMAS, F.L.S.

Author of "Tank Angling in India." MADRAS CIVIL SERVICE, RETIRED.

THIRD EDITION, revised, with numerous full-page and other Illustrations.

"A book to read for pleasure at home, as well as to use as a handbook of exceeding value to the angler who may be already there, or intending to visit India." *Land and Water.*

Foolscap 8vo., Cloth, 3/6.

Medical Hints for Hot Climates

And for those out of reach of Medical Aid.

BY

CHAS. HEATON, M.D.

"The title of this work is sufficiently explanatory of its nature. It is what it pretends to be—a portable book of medical reference, with plain practical hints and advice for people residing at out-stations or travelling in hot climates where skilled medical aid is not readily available for the treatment of emergent sickness or injury." *Lancet.*

INDIA.

Published Monthly. Subscription £1 1s. per annum.

Indian Medical Gazette.

A Record of Medicine, Surgery, and Public Health, and of Genera Medical Intelligence, Indian and European.

Edited by Surgn.-Capt. C. H. BEDFORD, D. Sc., M.D.
Associate-Editors Surgn.-Lt.-Col., J. Maitland, M.D., Madras
Surgn.-Lt.-Col. W. K. HATCH, M.D., Bombay.

Crown 8vo., Cloth, 10/6.

The Management and Medical Treatment of Children in India.

BY

EDWARD A. BIRCH, M.D., Surgeon-Major Bengal Establishment.

THIRD EDITION.

Enlarged and Revised (1895), *with additional Chapter on Poisons.*

"This is the third edition of Dr. Birch's version of Goodeve's 'Hints,' and has spared no pains to bring it into line with the most recent views and practic regarding the hygienic medical treatment of infants and children."—*British Medic Journal.*

Crown 8vo., 4/6.

The Indian Cookery Book.

A Practical Handbook to the Kitchen in India adapted to the Thre Presidencies.

BY

A THIRTY-FIVE YEARS' RESIDENT.

Containing Original and Approved Recipes in every department of India Cookery; Recipes for Summer Beverages and Home-made Liquers; Medicinal an other Recipes; together with a variety of things worth knowing.

INDIA.

Pocket-Book Form, Cloth, 4/6.

Permanent Way Pocket-Book.

Containing complete Formulæ for Laying Points, Crossings, Cross-over Roads, Through Roads, Diversions, Curves, etc., suitable for any Gauge.

BY

T. W. JONES.

WITH ILLUSTRATIONS.

Crown 8vo., 16/-.

Hindu Castes and Sects.

An Exposition of the Origin of the Hindu Caste System and the Bearing of the Sects towards each other and towards other Religious Systems.

BY

JOGANDRA NATH BHATTACHARYA, M.A., D.L.

"To those who are interested in the history and philosophy of religions, and especially to those who are making a study of the religious customs of the East, this book will prove both welcome and useful; not perhaps for its own sake alone but also for its suggestiveness."—*Home News.*

Imperial 16mo., Cloth, 10/6.

Hindu Mythology.

Vedic and Puranic.

BY

W. J. WILKINS, of the London Missionary Society, Calcutta.

PROFUSELY ILLUSTRATED.

"His aim has been to give a faithful account of the Hindu deities such as an intelligent native would himself give, and he has endeavoured, in order to achieve his purpose, to keep his mind free from prejudice or theological bias. The author has attempted a work of no little ambition and has succeeded in his attempt, the volume being one of great interest and usefulness."—*Home News.*

INDIA.

Royal 8vo., Boards, 7/6.

THACKER'S

Directory of the Chief Industries of India, 1898.

WITH WHICH IS INCORPORATED

A LIST OF TEA COMPANIES AND GARDENS,

INDIGO AND COFFEE ESTATES, WITH THEIR FACTORY MARKS;

AND A

DIRECTORY OF TEA, COFFEE, CINCHONA,

AND

CARDAMOM ESTATES IN CEYLON, WITH TWO MAPS.

CONTENTS.

Breweries, Carpet Manufactories, Cinchona, Coal Mines, Coffee (India and Ceylon), Cotton Mills and Presses, Dairy Farms, Distilleries, Flour Mills, Gold Mines, Ice Companies, Indigo, Iron Works, Jute Presses and Mills, Lac, Orchards, Paper Mills, Petroleum, Potteries, Quarries, Rice Mills, Roperies, Salt, Saw Mills, Silk, Sugar, Tea Companies and Gardens in India and Ceylon, Tobacco, Wool, etc.

PUBLISHED ANNUALLY.

THACKER'S SIX SHILLING SERIES—*continued.*

Jason Edwards.

BY

HAMLIN GARLAND.

* *Other Works by this Author are in preparation.*

The Tribes on my Frontier.

BY

E. H. AITKEN.

SIXTH EDITION.

With Fifty Illustrations by F. C. Macrae.

Behind the Bungalow.

BY

E. H. AITKEN.

Fifth Edition. Illustrated by F. C. Macrae.

A Naturalist on the Prowl.

BY

E. T. AITKEN.

SECOND EDITION.

Illustrated by a series of 80 Drawings by R. A. Sterndale.

The Captain of the "Mary Rose."

BY

W. LAIRD CLOWES.

Author of "The Naval Pocket Book," &c.

ILLUSTRATED.

Twenty-One Days in India.

BY

GEORGE ABERIGH-MACKAY.

A NEW EDITION.

Illustrated by the Author.

∴ *New Works are constantly being added to this Series.*